THE NEXT
FOUR YEARS

THE NEXT FOUR YEARS

A Vision of Victory

Howard Phillips

Adroit Press
Franklin, Tennessee

Legacy Commications   Policy Analysis, Inc.
P.O. Box 680365   9520 Bent Creek Lane
Franklin, Tennessee 37068   Vienna, VA 22182

ISBN: 0-9633469-3-8

CONTENTS

FOREWORD

Joseph Sobran

D o conservatives want to put another Republican—even a Reagan—in the White House?

I ask this question because the Republican pattern has been to consolidate the accumulated gains of the Democrats, never threatening, much less seriously attempting, to repeal them. The federal government continued to grow under Reagan, and got an extra boost from Bush. What will be the point of replacing Clinton with a Republican who at best will play goalie, but won't try to score?

Howard Phillips, running for President on the U.S. Taxpayers Party ticket, thinks it's time conservatives got serious about rescinding the Great Society, the New Deal, the Federal Reserve System, and the personal income tax. In other words, he has a conservative agenda that is more ambitious than blocking the next liberal initiative, while coming up with "market-based" conservative versions of them (such as enterprise zones, "private" health care plans, etc.). He wants to restore the U.S. Constitution.

Even conservatives are in the habit of thinking like liberals in some respects. As Phillips puts it, they ask for half a loaf as a bargaining position, serving notice that they will settle for less. Meanwhile, radical groups like organized homosexuals demand the whole loaf, and despite their small numbers and the revulsion they inspire, wind up getting most of what they want. The failure of the conservative approach is evident everywhere, but most discouragingly in the recent abortion ruling of the Supreme Court—eight of whose members have been appointed by Republican presidents. (The sole exception, Byron White, a Kennedy appointee, has been on the side of the angels.)

Without endorsing Bill Clinton, Phillips points out that when we have a liberal Republican in the White House, we get two liberal parties in Congress—because even most conservative Republican congressmen will vote with the President out of party loyalty. And as Michael Kinsley gleefully observes, Bush *is*, in effect, a liberal. The only reason liberals oppose him, after vast spending increases, tax increases, a Clean Air act, a handicapped rights bill, and a racial quota bill, is that he hasn't quite given them *everything* they want. They aren't half-a-loafers.

Both the *New York Times* and the *Washington Post* have run recent front-page articles on the alleged problem of "gridlock" in Washington. It seems that not enough legislation is passing, because the White House and Congress can't cooperate. Tacit message: We need Clinton.

But note the assumption that we somehow need more and more laws. Passing laws is a good thing in itself. The government's job is to keep legislating incessantly. Like the empty slogan of "change," the cry of "gridlock" is thoughtless—or it's an attempt to induce thoughtlessness in readers. What the two great liberal dailies are lamenting is really checks and balances. Never mind that every law constricts our freedom a little more, and that enough laws will leave us with no freedom at all. That people can talk this way even now is an awful comment on the quality of the Republican leadership we have had for so many years.

The whole loaf we should be fighting for is a conservative Congress whose chief business will be chopping down the jungle of bad laws that oppress us, laws that range from misconceived to iniquitous and unconstitutional. The real opposite of a legislating party is not a foot-dragging party, but a party of repeal.

We may as well get started. Phillips has the foresight to see what is needed, even though it doesn't exist yet. In time others will come to see it, too. He has been working hard to build something, even while nobody was paying attention, while George Bush looked unbeatable, while Ross Perot was the national sensation. He has not only kept the faith, he has supplemented his fortitude with great political insight. I myself am just beginning to realize things he appreciated long ago, and I admire him immensely. He deserves millions of votes, and I regret that I can only give him one. But I won't feel that that one is wasted. I will feel that it has been consecrated to something worthy.

ACKNOWLEDGMENTS

The great opportunity we have today to redeem our heritage of liberty would not have come to pass without the sacrificial efforts of thousands of people all over America who have—without one penny of taxpayer funding or government subsidy—worked hard to lay the foundations for our new political party and to qualify its candidates for the ballot, whether by petition or primary victory or convention. They come from states all over America—from Michigan to Mississippi, from Maine to Minnesota, from Iowa to Arkansas, from Nevada to New Jersey, from California to South Carolina, from Massachusetts to Utah, from Tennessee and Kentucky to Alaska and Washington State, from Rhode Island to Louisiana, from Nebraska to New Mexico, from Wisconsin to Vermont.

It's impossible to acknowledge everyone at this time, but let me express particular gratitude to those whose successful efforts were far above and beyond the call of duty:

Mark Weaver, without whom there would be no U.S. Taxpayers Party.

Dan Hansen, Chuck Horne, Lucille Lusk, Janine Hansen, and all the leaders of Nevada's Independent American Party.

Dr. Was Krogdahl and the dedicated members of the Kentucky Taxpayers Party.

Trent Galloway and his colleagues in the Arkansas Taxpayers Party.

Dr. Randy Bragdon and his wonderful family in the great state of Maine.

Patricia Manning, Alfred Fiske, Joe Devine, and all of our other friends in Rhode Island.

Lucille Brandt, whose hard work qualified our ticket for the ballot in Wisconsin.

The wonderful Woltmann family of Minnesota: may their numbers multiply.

Supreme Court Justice Bill Goodloe of the Washington Taxpayers Party and his son, Richard, and Todd Richert, who has done such a great job in helping us build that party.

And, of course, Bill and Eileen Shearer and all of our faithful friends in the great American Independent Party of California, which this year is celebrating its silver anniversary.

I want to thank Karl Falster, and Jackie Pierce, and Curtis Caine, and all the Mississippi Taxpayers Party as well as Jack Phelps in Alaska; Bob Tisch, Joe Sanger, John Pafford, and all the other members of the Tisch Independent Citizens Party of Michigan; Don Rogers in the state of Utah, David Rockett and Jim Ware, in the state of Louisiana; the John Diaz family, as well as Lowell and Dixie Lee Patterson in New Jersey; Ted Adams and his wonderful wife, Bonnie, and Robert Clarkson of the South Carolina American Party; George Grant, Mary Jane Morris, Mark Horne, W. Z. Baumgartner, and the other leaders of the Tennessee Taxpayers Party; Ron Brown of the New Mexico Taxpayers Party; Warren Larson in Nebraska; Len Umina of the Independent Voters Party in Massachusetts, and all of our good friends—Chris Olson, Sam Blumenfeld, and others from Massachusetts; Verla Maxfield and Mark Hepworth, who did such a great job in the state of Iowa. And *so many more*, not least among them Jeff Baker and our friends in the great state of Florida, who collected some 80,000 signatures for a candidate who was much less than a household word.

I thank each and every one of you—those who succeeded and those who did not. I thank those who *have*, and those who *will*. Those who were at our inaugural convention, and those who couldn't be with us on that historic occasion.

I also want to thank all of the great speakers at our convention, beginning with my wise counsellor, the great R. J. Rushdoony, and our magnificent keynoter, Otto Scott.

What a grand coalition has been represented here: Jack Gargan of THRO, who launched the Draft Ross Perot movement more than a year ago. Ron Paul, who was the Libertarian presidential nominee for whom I voted in 1988, and Congressman Bill Dannemeyer, the conscience of the Republican Party in the United States House of Representatives. I appreciate each and every one of our other speakers: Emmanuel McLittle, George Grant, Ed Vieira, and one of America's very greatest ambassadors, David Funderburk of North Carolina.

I want to thank another man who was not at the convention, Rus Walton of the Christian Committees of Correspondence, who, together with Tim Duskin and Al Knight, did such a tremendous job in crafting a platform which, I think, is superior to any other I have ever seen.

Let me especially thank my family for the support they have provided and the sacrifices in which they have shared: my wife, Peggy; my daughter, Alexandra; my son, Sam—and my other children: Doug and his wife, Beall; Amanda, her husband, Brian, and our grandson, Ben; and our son, Brad, and our daughter, Jenny. I especially thank my mother, in Massachusetts—the great Bay State where I was nurtured and born.

PUBLISHER'S INTRODUCTION

This is a book about change—change for the better.

We are living at a time when the frustrations of the citizenry seem to be at an all-time high. Uncertainty runs rampant. No area of life seems exempt from a looming sense of dread. The doom-and-gloom rhetoric of the professional socio-political soothsayers has finally permeated the masses. Thus, second-guessing foreign policy decisions has become almost second-nature. The collapse of Communism and the redrawing of the map of Europe—once the cause for joyous celebration—has raised disturbing new questions about the stability of our world. And the looming specter of Japanese strength has sent ominous signals around the globe.

Meanwhile here at home, the economy is perceived as unstable, at best. The federal deficit has grown to Babylonian proportions. The tax burden continues to weigh heaviest on the average citizen. The integrity of the family is sorely threatened. Educational standards have utterly collapsed. Crime and violence seem to be raging out of control. Scandal and corruption have compromised the foundational institutions of faith, politics, and charity. Racial tensions have once again erupted in our inner cities. Abortion, environmentalism, radical feminism, AIDS, pornography, drug abuse, and homosexual activism have fragmented and polarized our communities. The basic values of our nation are now persistently called into question. Patriotism has very nearly succumbed to cynicism. And in the midst of this long litany of woe, public distrust of government is epidemic—while public distrust of government officials and wanna-be government officials is pandemic.

By all accounts, politics as usual simply will not be sufficient to wrench us out of our cultural malaise. People are ready for change. They want answers. They yearn for a voice of reason. They are tired of the hype, the hyperbole, and the hypocrisy. They have lost patience. They want to see action. In fact, throughout most of the 1992 campaign season, it seemed as if the favorite presidential candidate of the majority of Americans was "none of the above." Voters seemed to be caught in the nether realm between the languor of sheer electoral pragmatism and the lassitude of a lesser-of-evils abnegation.

As a result, this may very well be one of the most bizarre political episodes in our nation's history. The common wisdom has been utterly confounded time after time. According to John Sununu, "We may need a whole new vocabulary to describe the oddities of the political twists and turns of the nineties." Michael Kinsley agrees saying, "I've practically run out of words to describe the strange events of this political conundrum."

Since the entrenchment of the two-party system in America, independent or third-party candidates for federal office traditionally have not done terribly well. Theodore Roosevelt ran the last genuinely viable third-party presidential race back in 1912. And despite his overwhelming coast-to-coast popularity, he lost—while simultaneously destroying the reelection chances for the Republican incumbent, Howard Taft. But as the Perot phenomenon has shown, historical precedent may not be the most telling factor in the decade to come. This could very well be the time of a kind of political *Aquarius* when an independent *Jupiter* aligns with the *Mars* of voter discontent.

Stranger things have happened.

Recognizing that fact, a group of concerned citizens, community leaders, public officials, political theorists, and grassroots activists gathered in New Orleans on September 4–5, 1992 for an historic meeting: the first national convention of the U.S. Taxpayers Party (USTP). This book is a collection of the speeches that they gave and the platform that they drafted.

The contributors include some of the most prominent names in the modern conservative movement:

- **Howard Phillips,** chosen by the convention to represent the USTP as its first presidential candidate, has a record of overcoming great odds to achieve results. As director of the U.S. Office of Economic Opportunity (OEO), he fought to end the use of Federal funds as ideological patronage for the radical Left. Married, with six children, Phillips, age 51, has been the chairman of The Conservative Caucus since 1974. A 1962 graduate of Harvard College, where he was twice elected student council president, Phillips was chairman of the Boston Republican Party from 1964–1966. He has led national campaigns to aid anti-communist freedom fighters, to defeat anti-defense disarmament treaties with Moscow, to deploy the Strategic Defense Initiative (SDI), and to dramatically reduce Federal taxes, spending, and regulation.

- **Brig. General Albion Knight** has more than thirty years experience in nuclear weapons policy as well as in logistics and communications. He has served in key management nuclear weapons positions in the Army, Department of Defense, Atomic Energy Commission, and the Energy Research and Development Administration (ERDA). General Knight resigned from ERDA in protest over President Carter's arms control policies. Since then he has written and spoken widely against unilateral disarmament, appeasement, and trading with the enemy. He has also been an ordained clergyman since 1954. He was chosen as the Presidential running mate of Howard Phillips.

- **Congressman William Dannemeyer** has been described as "the conscience of the Republican Party in the U.S. House of Representatives," for his leadership against the militant homosexual and abortion lobbies.

- **George Grant** is the author of more than a dozen books on politics, social issues, and history, including critical biographies of H. Ross Perot and Hillary Rodham-Clinton as well as exposés of Planned Parenthood, the American Civil Liberties Union, and the radical environmentalist movement. He has been a leader in the pro-life movement for the last two decades.

- **Otto J. Scott,** a freelance writer and Chalcedon Foundation associate, is a biographer and historian. He has written books on James I, Robespierre, and John Brown. A former oil company and ad agency executive, he has lived in South American and travelled widely. He once served as Senior Editor of *Conservative Digest* magazine.

- **Emanual McLittle** is the publisher of *Destiny* magazine. McLittle attended the University of Detroit, was educated as a psychologist, but turned editor in an effort to produced the country's first widely distributed magazine for black conservatives.

- **Edwin Vieira, Jr.,** author of *Pieces of Eight,* a history of constitutional money, is a graduate of Harvard College and Harvard Law School. He also earned a Ph.D. in chemistry from Harvard University.

- **David B. Funderburk** was U.S. Ambassador to Romania from 1981 to 1985. In 1985 he resigned in protest against the U.S. State Department's support of Communist Dictator Nicolai Ceausescu. Since then he has written *Pinstripes and Reds* and *Betrayal of America.*

- Elected to represent his south Texas district in Congress four times, **Dr. Ron Paul** was the 1988 Libertarian Party presidential nominee. In addition, he is a practicing physician and a prolific author.

- **R. J. Rushdoony** is a prolific writer and one of America's most influential theologians today. He is president of the Chalcedon Foundation and the author of more than thirty books on philosophy, theology, and world and American history.

- **John J. "Jack" Gargan** is the founder of T.H.R.O. (Throw the Hypocritical Rascals Out) who launched the Anti-incumbent movement in 1990.

It is clear from their speeches assembled here—as well as from the platform that follows—that these men do not hold utopian aspirations for the restoration of the great American experiment in liberty. They fully recognize that maintaining liberty is hard. It requires something of us. Of all of us. The institutional hedges that afford us freedom necessitate a certain level of upkeep. They require both diligence and vigilance.

The doctrine of the *separation of powers* is a cherished constitutional concept whereby each of the *separate* branches of government maintains *separate* authorities, *separate* jurisdictions, and *separate* functions. This kind of separation is the practical keystone for another hallowed constitutional concept: the doctrine of *checks and balances*. Theoretically, the judicial, legislative, and executive branches are to restrain one another from inordinate influence. The Founding Fathers saw the separation of powers—and its corollary checks and balances—as essential for the maintenance of freedom in their nascent experiment in liberty.

But they were not new or original ideas. The notion of separate powers and the imposition of checks and balances did not suddenly dawn on Washington, Adams, Madison, Hamilton, Jay, and Morris. Nor were they unique to those men's mentors: Rutherford, Cromwell, Witherspoon, Smith, and Locke. Instead, the doctrines come straight out of the American cultural tradition of decentralized responsibility.

Interestingly though, the idea of distinct jurisdictions and balanced institutions is not limited in that long and venerable tradition simply and solely to the area of civil government. According to that unique perspective, the family, the community, and even the church are divinely established institutions right alongside the state. Each of them has its own authority, its own jurisdiction, and its own function. Each of them is a *separate* power. And each of them is to hold in check and weigh in balance each of the others.

What that means is that separation of powers and checks and balances are not simply functions of state action. Instead, they are to be carried out in contradistinction to the state by the family, the community, and the church. To center all the cultural power and activity around politics and state is nothing more than *statism*.

Even those conservatives who spend all their time and energy trying to *limit* the size and influence of the state are ultimately statist because their whole worldview is centered in the political realm. They are statists struggling for a small limited state, while liberals are struggling for a large universal state. But they are both statist. The fact is that all men who break with the American tradition of a balanced, multi-jurisdictional culture are ultimately statists, because they have nowhere else to turn to establish life, liberty, and the pursuit of happiness than the state.

The traditional American perspective of social transformation is *personal*. It includes politics. It includes vibrant and decisive leadership. It includes influencing local government, legislators, the executive branch, the judiciary, and the bureaucracy. It includes grassroots mobilization, revitalized civic accountability, and committed community caucusing. It includes all these things. But it includes a whole lot more. That whole lot more is not statist—centered in and around a single sovereign institution. It is personal. It is separated out among, and balanced between, several decentralized institutions and the people that compose them.

Ultimately, that means that there are no easy answers. Not in mere ideology. Not in mechanical quick fixes. Not in alluring leadership. Not even in the establishment of new movements, coalitions, or parties. Instead, the restoration of our republic will come when we do the hard work—the vigilant work—of preserving liberty one person at a time, one family at a time, one community at a time, and one church at a time.

George Washington, in one of his final statements to the young nation that he had taken such a pivotal role in establishing, said:

I now make it my earnest prayer, that God would most graciously be pleased to dispose us all, to do justice, to love mercy, and to demean ourselves with that charity, humility, and pacific temper of mind, which were the characteristics of the Divine Author of our blessed religion, for without an humble imitation and example in these things, we can never hope to be a happy nation.

He understood only too well that in order to secure life, liberty, and the pursuit of happiness in this land, a foundation had to be laid first—a foundation rooted in personal commitment and responsibility.

That takes work. Hard work.

And that is what the U.S. Taxpayers Party and the contributors to this volume offer: the opportunity to work hard over the next four years to restore this republic to its once firm foundations in every realm and in every jurisdiction of life and culture.

1. WE CLAIM THE FUTURE

Howard Phillips

*E*ach of us has much for which to be thankful. God has put us in this place at this time for purposes we may not yet fully comprehend.

But this much we do know: Our country is in crisis because it has departed from the Biblical faith, the common law principles, and the constitutional requirements which enabled the American nation to become the most blessed in all recorded history.

The Republicans in the White House and the Democrats in the Congress have compounded the crisis, squandered the heritage, and opened the door to disasters which have corrupted our country and added to the burdens afflicting every American family.

Economically, America is headed for disaster. Unless we change the policies of the Republican White House and the Democrat Congress, every American family will, in this decade, be impoverished by a hyperinflationary depression which shreds our savings, junks our jobs, and requires each of us to labor longer for reduced rewards.

During the past twelve years, under budgets proposed and signed by Ronald Reagan and George Bush, and approved by the Democrats in Congress, our national debt—which, through nearly 200 years of history, had been held to less than one trillion dollars—has *quadrupled*, increased by a factor of four, from $914 billion in 1981 to $4.1 trillion today. Last year, 1991, it took $306 billion simply to pay the interest on the national debt.

We paid $468 billion in income taxes last year. If we don't turn around the debt, or at least stop adding to it, in a few years, when interest rates are back at record high levels, it will cost more to service the debt than can possibly be collected from income taxes, *even* at their present burdensome levels.

In 1987, the federal government spent one trillion dollars. That was only five years ago. Now, George Bush has proposed a $1.5 trillion budget, 50 percent bigger than it was just five years ago. Mr. Bush has even recommended a one-year deficit of $400 billion.

That is a little bit out of whack for a president who has attacked his opponents for opposing his Balanced Budget Amendment.

We know that Dan Quayle can't spell, but that's not nearly so serious as the fact that George Bush cannot add.

He has multiplied our problems; he has subtracted from our strength; he has divided us from our dollars; but he cannot add.

If he *could* add, Mr. Bush would see that, at his present rate of growth in spending and debt, the national debt will be in the neighborhood of 6 or 7 trillion dollars if we give him four more years. My friends, that's a very expensive neighborhood. And we will be paying more in interest than they will be taking from us in income taxes.

That's a recipe for ruin, a budget bound for bankruptcy.

The laws of gravity apply to America as well as to other nations—so do the laws of economics.

If our so-called leaders are so locked into the special interests which finance their campaigns that they will not cut spending, and if they can't squeeze out any more from us in taxes (on the principle that you can't get blood from a stone), and if it's not time to sell off the government's assets—then they have only two choices left: they can borrow more money and increase the burden of debt on ourselves and our posterity, *or* they can devalue the dollars we have earned and saved by printing more Federal Reserve Notes—purporting to create value with the push of a button on their printing press.

If you and I printed greenbacks purporting to represent real value, but with nothing to back them up, we would be called counterfeiters—and the charge would be accurate. But, somehow, our politicians think that election to office gives them a license to steal. Their counterfeiting may have official approval, but that does not undo the damage, or make things any better for the victims.

The ability of the federal government to borrow more money to cover its debts is sharply declining. All over the world, those who understand simple arithmetic have learned that the "full faith and credit" of the U.S. government is not what it used to be.

And even as the lending windows close, the dollar is sinking dramatically to new lows against the Deutschmark and other currencies.

It used to be that no matter how many dollars the Fed printed, they would be eagerly sought out all over the world—whether by drug dealers in Columbia or by black marketeers in Moscow.

But, now, as the dollarization of the world is ended by the escalation of America's debt, we will feel the full effect of inflation here at home, especially after November, when interest rates begin climbing back to higher levels.

I'm 51 years old. Four decades ago I could pay twenty-five cents and see a double feature at the neighborhood movie house. Today, one movie would likely cost about five dollars.

Believe me, it's not that movies are better. They're not. It's simply that dollars buy less. Today's dollar is worth one-twentieth of what it was forty years ago.

And, unless we throw out the two-party, special-interest, Republicrat monopoly control of our government, it may be only four *years*, not four *decades*, before the dollar is reduced yet again to one-twentieth of its prior value.

Since 1961, when John F. Kennedy took office some 30 years ago, annual federal spending has increased astronomically, from less than $100 billion to more than $1.5 trillion this year.

Income taxes have been raised from $41 billion per year in 1961 to nearly half a trillion dollars this year. Social Security taxes have been raised from $12 billion per year in 1961 to $370 billion last year—that is an increase by a factor of 30! People last year paid 30 times as much in Social Security taxes as they had paid in the 1961 year, thirty years previous.

What a burden that is on the American working man and woman! What a burden that is on the American family! What a burden that is on small business!

Is it any wonder, with all of these taxes and all of this regulation, that we have so much unemployment? Is it any wonder that businesses are reluctant to hire more employees? That, instead of giving people the advantage of benefits and health insurance, they're going to consultants, or they're leasing their employees, or they're reducing their objectives and lowering their horizons.

Taxes on employers have been raised from $21 billion in 1961 to $96 billion 30 years later.

Government does not produce wealth: it consumes it, squanders it, and redistributes it.

As our platform says: it's still theft, even if it's done in broad daylight, in elegant surroundings, by majority vote.

There are several questions we must ask ourselves: Is America better off because of all the additional taxes, spending, and regulation of the past thirty years?

Are we better off because so much of our earnings and savings are transferred each day from our pockets to those who act in our *name*, but not in our *behalf*, in Washington, D.C.?

Are our streets safer?

Is our industrial base stronger?

Have the nation's morals been uplifted?

Can our politicians spend our own money more wisely than we can? The answers are NO, NO, NO, NO, and NO.

Crime and unemployment are up. Jobs and prosperity are down. The culture has been corrupted. And sodomy is subsidized with our taxes.

The U.S. Taxpayers Party has a plan which is as sound as it is simple and straightforward.

We want to roll the clock back 30 years on taxes, on spending, and on regulation. And we want to roll it back 200 years to the principles of liberty which were incorporated in America's founding documents.

The Tenth Amendment to the Constitution—which punctuated our Bill of Rights—sets forth explicitly that "The powers not delegated to the United States by the Constitution, nor prohibited by it to the States, are reserved to the States respectively, or to the people."

In plain English, if it's not in the Constitution, then neither our politicians, our bureaucrats, not even our judges, can lawfully take our money or regulate our activities.

Furthermore, Article I Section 9 of that same Constitution makes clear that funds may be expended from the federal treasury in only two ways: Congress can pass a money bill and the President can sign it, or Congress can pass a money bill, the President can veto it, and his veto can be overridden by two-thirds of the members in each house of Congress. Otherwise, the money cannot be spent.

In the first budget I will send to Congress as President of the United States, I will propose spending cuts of $500 billion, and tax cuts of like amount, achieved by eliminating the individual income tax and abolishing the Internal Revenue Service.

If Congress sends me any other budget, I will veto it. If my veto is overridden, I will go to the American people on national television—even if we have to buy the cameras—and I will ask them to vote in the 1994 congressional elections only for candidates, regardless of party, who publicly pledge to sustain my tax and spending vetoes in the next meeting of the Congress of the United States.

All we will need to succeed is one-third plus one of the members of one house of Congress (that's 34 Senators, or 145 of 435 Representatives). We can govern with *one President and one-third plus one* of one house of Congress. That is the new political math for political reform in the 1990s.

Once voters have accepted our Grand Bargain, and are no longer required to pay income taxes—and, of course, that Grand Bargain is $500 billion less spending and $500 billion less in taxes—then we will move immediately to a balanced budget, privatizing or cancelling government programs which did not exist thirty years ago and/or which are not explicitly authorized under the Constitution of the United States.

We will no longer be required to waste 25 billion of our tax dollars per year on an unconstitutional federal Department of Education, or $23 billion for the federal Department of Housing and Urban Development.

I didn't like HUD very much when Lyndon Johnson created it, and I don't like it any better when it's spending a lot more money under the leadership of our friend, Jack Kemp. It's still a bad idea, and it's got to go!

We'll no longer be required to waste $12 billion on the International Monetary Fund, which is a laundering agency for our tax dollars which are sent overseas to socialist governments so they can repay their bad loans from the big international banks.

We will no longer unconstitutionally waste $18 billion on foreign aid, or $176 million on the National Endowment for the Arts, or $350 million on the Legal Services Corporation, or $5.1 billion on taxpayer-guaranteed grain sales to Moscow, or $4.9 billion to fulfill the political agenda of the militant homosexual movement.

This is worth working for.

We will pay the legitimate costs of government with a constitutional tariff, proceeding from the premise enunciated by Abraham Lincoln: that tariffs on foreign companies and products are preferable to taxes on American businesses and workers.

To the extent that there is a shortfall, we will share the burden among the fifty states, with each state responsible for raising a share of revenues equivalent to its share of the national population. That will change the political dynamic—with states learning to demand less, rather than more, federal spending.

And we will fight both inflation and debt by abolishing the unconstitutional authority of the Federal Reserve system, which puts ink on paper and calls it money. We will instead restore the system set forth in the Constitution, wherein, just as the yardstick has 36 inches of undiminished value seven days every week, so will the dollar have 100 cents of unmanipulated worth seven days every week.

In the process, we will look forward to a time when the dollar will once again be as good as gold, and when bankers behind the scenes are stripped of authority to increase their wealth by adding to our debt.

In foreign policy, we reject the New World Order of George Bush, Bill Clinton, and their colleagues in the Trilateral Commission and the Council on Foreign Relations.

Harking back to the principle enunciated by John Quincy Adams (another Massachusetts boy), we will be the friend of liberty everywhere, but the guarantor and provisioner of ours alone.

We will not have our wealth sent abroad to underwrite the bad loans of international banks or the business risks of multi-national corporations.

We will fight no war except to defend the proximate vital interests of the United States of America, and our troops will serve under no flag except the Stars and Stripes.

And when we do go to war, we shall do so in accordance with the Constitution—not by unilateral preemptive executive action, but by declaration of the people's representatives in the United States Congress.

One thing more: we will not send our mothers and daughters, our wives and sisters, to fight our wars.

At the same time, we commit ourselves to provide for the common defense, and to reject the unilateral disarmament of our military-industrial infrastructure. We also point out that, that which is hastily destroyed will be difficult to quickly rebuild.

For that reason I oppose the 25 to 30 percent reduction in U.S. military strength, which has been promoted both by the Democrats in Congress and the Republicans in the White House.

The job of the President and the Congress is to evaluate, not merely the perceived present intentions of actual adversaries, but, more importantly, to prepare for the potential capabilities which others may possess later in this decade.

To that end, I would restrict the transfer of United States technology, move forward with our space program, and act immediately, on my first day in office, to fully develop and deploy SDI by giving the requisite six months' notice, beginning on that first day, for withdrawal from the Nixon-Brezhnev ABM treaty of 1972.

That treaty has prevented America and American presidents and an American Congress from defending us against potential nuclear attack—whether from a reborn Russian imperialism, a residual Cuban tyranny, or an ongoing terrorist threat.

America's crises are also institutional and moral, not merely economic and strategic. We must use the authority granted by the Constitution to the Congress and the president to control the purse-strings and clip the wings of a judicial branch which regards its own *opinions*, rather than the plain language of the United States Constitution, as the law of the land. We must challenge the presumptuous and malignant tyranny of arrogant judges who uphold abortion, even as they seek to prohibit prayer.

Using the authority of Article III of the Constitution, we shall limit their jurisdiction, overturn their usurpations, and return the power to apprehend, prosecute, convict, and execute criminals to the cities and towns all over America where the crimes occur, and to ordinary men and women, who may not have law degrees from Ivy League institutions, but who understand their duty to safeguard their families and their communities from rape, murder, and other forms of criminal assault.

America does not need more prisons, costing taxpayers as much for the upkeep of criminals as it would to send them to Harvard. What we do need are more executions of those who constitute a threat to the physical safety of the law-abiding, and more *restitution*, in accordance with which the perpetrators of crimes against property will be indentured to their victims rather than being made an ever greater burden on all the rest of us.

We must rein in a Congress which, even as it has provided for automatic increases in its own pay, inflated its pensions, and expanded its perquisites, has abrogated its responsibility to make law accountable to the people, instead permitting judges, civil servants, nonprofit corporations, regulatory agencies, and international bureaucracies, beyond accountability to the American electoral process, to exercise such authority in its stead— governing us without our consent.

The time has come to limit terms, to repeal pay raises, and to abolish pensions for elected officials (who are now financially rewarded for extending, rather than reducing their time in office). And we need to strengthen the role of the states in our federal system. A good way to begin is by working to repeal the 17th Amendment.

With each additional day in the District of Columbia, members of Congress forfeit ever more of their allegiance to the folks back home, and become citizens of a separate society in Washington, D.C., where political power is exercised and career advancement controlled, not by ordinary citizens, but by high-priced insider law firms, left-wing media manipulators, influential bankers, powerful corporate executives, and tax-funded special-interest groups.

As Jack Gargan has said: It's time to Throw the Hypocritical Rascals Out.

We do not come to spray perfume in the Augean stables, but to clean them out. We will not whitewash the Temples of Baal; we will tear them down.

There was once a time—unfortunately, beyond the memory of most of us—when the government of the United States fulfilled the Biblical mandate that it be a ministry of justice—and a terror to evil-doers.

The Framers acknowledged God as our Creator, our Lord, and the source of authority for all of our laws. They recognized that we were endowed by our Creator with certain rights which are inalienable—precisely because they are a gift from God, not a product of man's imperfect reason nor a beneficence from those who exercise political power.

We do not pledge our allegiance to a democracy—in which our rights to life, liberty, or property could be abridged or abolished—but to a republic, as guaranteed to each state in Article IV of the U.S. Constitution.

Our freedom of religion, guaranteed by the First Amendment, denies the federal government all authority to require that we subsidize any faith but our own. Our tax dollars may not constitutionally be authorized to underwrite the propagation of ideas we oppose.

Yet, even as President Bush asserts his allegiance to family values, he proposes and signs into law legislation which contradicts and undermines those values.

His appointees issue regulations and authorize subsidies to the anti-Christian enemies of every good thing he claims to uphold.

The abortion infrastructure in America is strengthened and subsidized by the $400 million of your tax dollars which George Bush sends to Planned Parenthood and its allies—at home and abroad— every year. And he's going to send them more next year, unless we stop it.

And it isn't the tooth fairy who uses hundreds of millions of your tax dollars to promote "safe sodomy"—by paying the overhead for the organizational infrastructure of the practitioners of anal intercourse and other perversions.

It is George Bush, the pro-family president.

It was not the Democratic Congress that proposed increasing the funding for the National Endowment for the Arts, and to extend it for five more years. It was George Bush.

America does not need a $176-million "ministry of culture" to shove down our throats perverse plays, performances, and posturings which have no real constituency except among those who steal our money to provide patronage for their "politically correct" friends who hate God, hate America, and even seem to hate themselves.

Let's tell the pro-family president that if he's such a big fan of blasphemy, pornography, and perversion, he should use his own money to pay for it—not ours.

And the same goes for PBS and NPR—national socialist radio—paid for with *your* tax dollars to establish a so-called "ministry of truth" to promote politically correct issues and opinions.

Under the First Amendment, those who differ with us are entitled to say what they think, but they aren't entitled to require us to subsidize the propagation of their ideas.

It truly is time for a change in America.

The train of civil government is heading over the cliff and taking all of us with it. It doesn't much matter whether we go over the cliff at 80 miles per hour with George Bush or 90 miles per hour with Bill Clinton.

We need to do more than change drivers. We need to change trains. And change directions.

That's why I thank God there is a brand new United States Taxpayers Party.

Today we are making history, launching a great new party which exists in every region of the country, built not with tax dollars, but by dedication and hard work.

This is the time—now is the hour—for us to formally begin the next step in our long journey—to reclaim our culture, to take back our government, to reconstruct our republic.

Since 1968 the Republicans have been capturing the presidency by campaigning as the anti-liberal party. But, in office, they have been the party that consolidated and expanded the Marxist agenda of Lyndon Johnson's Great Society.

When the Republicans control the White House, there are two liberal parties—and, until now, no conservative party.

Ted Kennedy wasn't able to pass his quota bill, until George Bush delivered the votes of all but five of the 43 Republicans in the U.S. Senate.

The brutalitarians in Red China could not get Most-Favored-Nation status until George Bush delivered three-fourths of the Republican senators to support it.

And furthermore, the militant homosexuals couldn't get their ADA bill—requiring restaurant owners to hire AIDS-infected homosexuals for food handling positions (if they are otherwise "qualified")—until George Bush lined up the Republican Party behind it.

The radical, anti-growth, anti-business, environmental socialists could not pass their so-called Clean Air Bill—costing us $40 billion per year—until George Bush pushed it through.

And the Democrats in Congress could not have raised our taxes to record high levels to pay for their socialist spending schemes without a liberal Republican president whose lying lips have revealed to us a lack of courage, an absence of character, and a shortage of principle.

And at his convention in Houston, just a couple of heatwaves from here, George Bush didn't even have the decency to forthrightly admit that he was wrong.

Instead of abjectly apologizing to the American people and begging for their forgiveness (as he should have done), George said: "The Democrats made me do it!" "The Congress made me do it!"

George Bush has a track record. Bill Clinton has a track record. And Howard Phillips has a track record.

I am the only candidate in this contest who, from start to finish, has refused to seek or accept taxpayer subsidies for his convention, or for his campaign. I intend to eliminate funding for the special interest groups—and to demonstrate my seriousness and sincerity of purpose, I must begin with my own special interest, as I have.

I am the only candidate, other than George Bush, who has ever headed a major federal agency: the United States Office of Economic Opportunity, OEO.

I learned in that job the hard facts about how our government has departed from its legitimate purposes.

More important, I learned what can be done using our great Constitution to put our government back on the right track. At OEO, I became a target for criticism as I sought to terminate discretionary federal grants and contracts which were being used as ideological patronage for virtually every faction and component of the radical left.

When President Nixon broke his pledge to veto further funding for the agency and its destructive, counterproductive, unconstitutional programs, I resigned from the federal government, and I've spent the past 19 years working as a private citizen and chairman of The Conservative Caucus, to take our government back.

Many of our good friends, despite the evidence that Republican politicians in office do not vote for or work for what their platforms sometimes promise and what we believe, continue to ask why we don't work through the Republican Party.

As a former chairman of the Republican Party in Boston, and a former assistant to the late, great Republican National Chairman Ray Bliss, I understand where they are coming from and respect their commitment to our philosophical cause, even as I reject their strategic conclusions.

The fact is the Republican Party is a house divided against itself. The workers oppose Planned Parenthood, "safe sodomy," high taxes, and the New World Order, but the leaders favor all of the above.

In the Republican Party, the conservatives get the platform, but the liberals get the government.

It is possible that someday a Pat Robertson or a Pat Buchanan or someone of their perspective might, indeed, capture a Republican presidential nomination. But, in order to unite their party, they would be required to surrender their agenda.

In this decade, the Republican Party is going to go the way of the Whigs in the 1850s. It will die the death of a double-minded man—who talks one way but lives in conflict with that which he professes to believe.

As in the 1850s, the decade when the Republican Party was born, we will witness, in this decade, the temporary displacement of our traditional two-party system.

We will also see three or more major parties on the scene by 1996—and we're going to be one of them. This will happen as voters and politicians seek to sort things out and once again produce a system which offers the American people real choices about the nation's direction.

In this context, it will be possible for us, or others, to capture a majority of the electoral college with only a plurality of the popular vote. That's how Lincoln became president in 1860. With less than 40 percent of the vote in a four-way contest, he earned a clear majority in the electoral college.

The other question we are asked is why voters should support us—at a time when the media studiously ignores or misrepresents our candidacy, and mention of us is omitted from the national opinion surveys.

My answer is that your vote is wasted only when you give it to someone who is leading the country away from what you believe. Bill Clinton and George Bush are two sides of the same devalued coin.

This party, our platform, and our candidates are committed to restoring America to its Biblical and constitutional premises.

Don't waste your vote on politicians who have lied to you before and will lie to you again.

Don't encourage them to think that "all is forgiven" when they haven't even asked for your forgiveness.

Instead, you and I ought to invest our votes in what we believe—we ought to give our votes to the candidates of the United States Taxpayers Party. I call on everyone to add to our strength with your votes. If you do so, you will strengthen that which you believe to be right and true, and you will hasten the day of our mutual victory.

For too long American conservatives have had as their objective "losing as slowly as possible." They've lived so long on crumbs from the Republican table that they think it's caviar.

It's time to reject the politics of "surrender on the installment plan," and to join us in raising up a new standard, in offering the American people a "vision of victory"—not a decade of despair, depression, and defeat.

As George Washington said at the Constitutional Convention in 1787, and as it is written on the masthead of the United States Taxpayers Alliance:

> If to please the people we offer what we ourselves disbelieve, how then may we afterward defend our work? Our job is to raise a standard to which the wise and honest may repair—recognizing that the event is in the hands of God.

I thank you for your friendship, your support, and for your nomination.

Your sacrificial efforts have brought us to this day.

Your prayers, your hard work, and your generous contributions enable us to continue with confidence.

Let us go forth with our strength renewed and our courage reinforced, offering hope that our children, and we as well, may once again live in a virtuous nation, blessed by God, striving humbly to serve His purposes, and rejoicing in His abundant blessings.

And let us now summon to our banner all who would join us to battle for the reconstruction of the American republic—and the restoration of these United States to our Biblical and constitutional heritage of liberty with freedom *under*—not freedom *from*—the laws of God.

My fellow Americans, we have made it to the starting gate.

Let the race begin!

2. A FREE AND INDEPENDENT REPUBLIC

Albion W. Knight, Jr.

*T*he nation truly faces a dire crisis. In addition to the serious economic dangers we face, the crisis also affects our safety and security. It is our duty in just such a crisis to demonstrate firm and unwavering resolve.

Our Founding Fathers created a republic whose people are entitled to make their own decisions about their well-being and future. For two centuries thereafter, the United States has prospered in freedom, justice, progress, and power as a sovereign independent nation, subject to no man-made laws other than those to which the American people have consented. Our state governments were committed to no interests but those of its free citizens and the republic of which they are a part.

Today, our republic faces profound dangers—not from foreign or domestic armies—but from immense power in the hands of political forces that openly seek to diminish or abolish our national sovereignty, independence, and integrity. The forces arise from leaders in government, the media, business, academia, and the church. They seek what they now call the "New World Order." President Bush does not seem to be able to define what that means—but it is a secular humanist vision of a "One World Government." For some it is the utopian dream of a peaceful world. For others it is a means of gaining power through an interlocking network of international financial and trade controlling agencies. We have both kinds in America.

Ever since Woodrow Wilson in 1913, our presidents have sought to grant more power to international agencies. This is especially true since World War II when the United Nations, the International Monetary Fund, and the World Bank were formed. Each time power is granted by our government to such agencies, decisions are transferred from the American taxpayer to international bureaucrats who are not subject to control by our Constitution and Congress. Yet this does not seem to bother our past eight presidents, especially George Bush. It does not bother Bill Clinton. Thus, if either man is elected, you can be sure that the New World Order will be one step closer to reality.

The Taxpayers Party affirms that *any* surrender of foreign policy or economic decision-making power to international agencies is not compatible with America's status as a sovereign nation. The Taxpayers Party says "NO" to the New World Order which will, in time, scrap the Declaration of Independence and the Constitution of the United

States. We say "YES" to the old American Republic. We refuse to condone passing *any* American sovereignty to *any* international agency. It is time to back away from the looming chasm of World government.

In order to preserve our republic, we support the following immediate actions:

1. The United States must withdraw from the United Nations and all of its agencies and activities. We shall ask the United Nations to find a new home elsewhere.

2. The United States must withdraw from all other international financial organizations which place critical economic decisions in the hands of foreign interests, individuals, organizations, businesses, or governments. This includes the International Monetary Fund, the World Bank, and the General Agreement on Tariffs and Trade.

As recommended by President George Washington in his Farewell Address, the United States should seek to live in peace and harmony with all nations. But we believe that quarrels between foreign nations are not a proper excuse for U.S. intervention. The United States is not and must not become a "World Policeman." Our government's duty is to defend the United States, not foreign countries or their interests.

Since World War II, the United States has given military and non-military aid to over 100 nations. Hundreds of billions of dollars have been poured down that bottomless pit—with little evident benefit to the safety and security of the American people. Not only have we given aid to our "friends," but to neutral nations whose "friendship" we hoped to buy. Now we are committing ourselves to send billions of American taxpayers' dollars to those who have been our enemies for years. This must stop! The U.S. government has no right, let alone any duty, to tax the American people to provide aid to foreign nations.

The Monroe Doctrine, announced in 1823, established the Western Hemisphere, especially Central America, as a priority interest to the United States. It is directly related to the safety and security of our nation. The Taxpayers Party reaffirms the importance of the Monroe Doctrine and proposes these actions:

1. Revoking of any agreements made in 1962 between President Kennedy and Khrushchev of the Soviet Union regarding the protection of Cuba. No longer will the U.S. Navy and U.S. Coast Guard protect Cuba from its freedom-seeking exiled patriots.

2. Recovery of complete control over the security and operation of the Panama Canal.

As a summary of our foreign policy objectives, we affirm that the vital interests of the American people must be of foremost importance to the U.S. government.

Each president has the responsibility to defend the American people from all dangers foreign and domestic. The world in the 1990s is no less dangerous than in the previous decades—it is in a most volatile, uncertain, and dangerous condition. Therefore, the United States must maintain a strong, modern and effective military and naval force. We wish all foreign leaders to think that the United States will fight to protect its vital interests and safety.

We remember the motto proclaimed on the first official American flag (the Rattlesnake flag raised by John Paul Jones): "Don't Tread on Me!" We also believe in the wisdom of Teddy Roosevelt who said that America should "Speak softly and carry a big stick." From the Bible comes the truth that a strong man armed keeps his goods in peace.

The Taxpayers Party, therefore, disagrees with the present drastic cut-back of our armed forces by the Congress in a feeding frenzy to gain more pork for their barrel. In so doing, they are playing fast and loose with the safety of the American people.

Defending our nation from nuclear attack by bombers and missiles has been a major concern of every president since the Soviet Union exploded their first atomic bomb. But for thirty years, the method of nuclear defense by our government under seven successive presidents has been one of the most immoral policies of any government in history. John Kennedy instituted an academic theory of deterrence called "mutual assured destruction" in which our own people were *intentionally* left undefended against missile or air attacks, while we threatened the other nations' populations (not their weapons) with nuclear destruction in retaliation after our own country would be in ashes. That policy's acronym is truthfully called "MAD"! In spite of President Reagan's Strategic Defense Initiative, which was never permitted to produce one defensive weapon, the present nuclear defense policy *still* depends upon the MAD doctrine. This is incredible when we know that, for over twenty years, we have had the technology for an effective defense against missiles.

The Taxpayers Party insists that the American *people* be protected and that the immoral theories of nuclear defense be placed in the scrap heap. Therefore, we shall:

1. Deploy an anti-missile defense system as soon as possible—with present technology— while continuing active development of improved systems.

2. Improve the nation's defense against air attack.

3. Abrogate President Nixon's 1972 ABM Treaty, which has been used by previous administrations as an excuse not to deploy an effective missile defense system.

Since 1958 every president has thought that nuclear defense could be gained by signing a series of disarmament treaties with the Soviet Union. Each treaty reduced our ability to defend our people, thus endangering America. What is appalling is that the Soviet Union cheated on every one of those agreements. What is worse is that our government *knew the Soviets cheated*, but still told the American people that they were being "protected" by these worthless pieces of paper.

The U.S. Taxpayers Party refuses to accept *any* previous disarmament treaty as being a valid means of protecting our people against foreign threats and dangers. Therefore we would cancel *all* disarmament treaties made with the Soviet Union or any other nation.

As a consequence of World War II, the United States made a number of alliances for the purpose of protecting Western civilization from the overwhelming military power of an aggressive Soviet Union. These alliances caused the deployment of American military forces on foreign soil for many years after World War II. They have been there too long. The alliances seem to have become permanent. But President Washington, further in his Farewell Address, gave us advice, which after two centuries is still wise:

> It is our true policy to steer clear of permanent alliances with any part of the foreign world. . . . Taking care always to keep ourselves by suitable establishments on a respectable defensive posture, we may safely trust to temporary alliances for extraordinary emergencies.

Therefore, the Taxpayers Party proposes to withdraw from the North Atlantic Treaty and remove our ground and air forces from the continent of Western Europe. Our European trade competitors are now able to defend themselves. We should remove our military forces from non-U.S. territory in the Pacific. Our Asian trade competitors should also assume the burden of their own security.

The United States must maintain the most modern program to explore space. This is important not only for our national security, but also for the continued exploitation of space for the economic well-being of our people. Therefore, the Taxpayers Party places a high priority on a healthy space program, both civilian and military.

The dangerous and unstable nature of the world requires the United States to maintain an effective intelligence capability. It must not only gather information about world conditions, but also provide the president and the Congress with an honest assessment of the meaning of those data, despite disagreements over the policies of the administration in power.

It is important, especially, to be able to assess what is happening in the former Soviet Union. While the Soviet Union may be gone, the Russian bear still has nuclear teeth. It still spies on the United States. Communists still cause trouble in the rest of the world. China is a growing nuclear threat to our safety. International terrorism remains a constant concern. Infiltration by foreign agents into the United States continues unabated. Yet, successive presidents since Nixon have reduced our intelligence capability when it is most needed. We must also restore our ability to detect those foreign agents working inside the United States.

Although we are concerned about other vitally important areas of national security, none are more disturbing than the possibility that Americans may still be alive and held as prisoners of war by our enemies. Under no condition is it morally correct for the United States government to delay *any* effort to return Americans home.

Clearly, the present pathway of foreign policy leads steadily toward the United States of America merging into a One World Government. This is totally unacceptable to the U.S. Taxpayers Party, and we know it is to all Americans who love their freedom. The principles of our Founding Fathers are still a good guide to preserve what they started: the United States as a free, sovereign, and independent republic. We in the Taxpayers Party will do all in our power to return to the well-worn pathways of those Fathers.

3. THE CULTURE WAR

Congressman William Dannemeyer

J ohn Gatto was given the "Most Outstanding Teacher" award in the city of New York in 1990. In accepting that great honor, he remarked:

> We live in a time of great social crisis. Our children rank at the bottom of 19 industrial nations in reading, writing and arithmetic. The world's narcotic economy is based upon our own consumption of this commodity. If we didn't buy so many powder dreams, the business would collapse, and schools are an important sales outlet. Our teenage suicide rate is the highest in the world, and suicidal kids are rich kids for the most part, not the poor. In Manhattan, 70 percent of all new marriages last less than five years.

Not a very pretty picture of the culture in America, no matter what our station in life. It troubles us all because we know intuitively as Americans that something is fundamentally wrong with this 200-year American experiment in self-government, and we're not quite sure what it is.

I am contrasting the Judeo-Christian culture that existed in this country under the Founding Fathers with what Mr. Gatto described, in order to begin to understand how we got to this point, and what steps we need to take to restore the greatness of America. In my judgment, we need to understand how to educate the next generation and how to correct some serious errors if we hope for our successors of hundred years from now to have the privilege of gathering together in the land of the free and the home of the brave (not the land of the *fee* and the home of the *slave*), to talk about freedom in America.

In colonial times, education was essentially done by the churches. When our Founding Fathers adopted the First Amendment to the Federal Constitution, it assumed those statements on human rights would be a beacon for the world. "Congress shall make no law respecting the establishment of a religion or prohibiting the free exercise thereof." They intended to forbid the federal government to establish a religion, knowing full well that the states had their own religions. Congregationalists were strong in New England, the Quakers in Pennsylvania, the Catholics in Maryland, and so on.

This is the way we educated the next generation. The *New England Primer*, which was in use at that time and for a hundred years following, acquainted children with the alphabet by referencing it with scriptural passages in order to inculcate them with the idea that the Bible has reference to their lives.

Like anything else in life, reformers come along and seek to change what is. This system of education was essentially in the hands of the religious communities until the mid-point of the last century, when it began to change. We began to see prophets come along saying, "Well now, we need to have public education developed in the country, separate and apart from the influence of the church because, well, things change," and that had a certain ring to it. In this century others could be named, but probably the most influential in terms of working to achieve this change was a man named John Dewey. He was an original signer of the Humanist Manifesto in 1933, which very simply says there is no God, there are no standards; you can do anything you want to, as long as you don't harm somebody else.

Dewey and his disciples set out to divorce the whole educational process from any influence of religion. He worked out of the Columbia School of Education in New York City, and was known as the father of progressive education. In a nutshell, he and his disciples have been successful beyond their fondest dreams in changing the culture of America. This movement has produced among certain cultural elites in this country disciples who follow the philosophy of secular humanism or moral relativism or atheism, whatever you want to call it.

Some of these elites are very powerful: the judiciary, academia, media, and political institutions such as the Democratic Party and People for the American Way.

Concerning the judiciary, Judge Robert Bork wrote an eloquent book called *The Tempting of America*, describing his experience seeking appointment to the U.S. Supreme Court. Atheism has infected the judiciary of this country. I'm not saying that the justices of our U.S. Supreme Court are evil or that they're devoid of any moral or religious sense themselves. I'm saying that they were influenced by the philosophy of John Dewey. This is reflected in the culture of which we are now a part, for better or for worse, beginning in 1962 with the decision of *Engle vs. Vitale,* when we knocked voluntary prayer out of public schools.

In 1973 under *Roe v. Wade,* in one of the most infamous decisions of this century, we set aside the law respecting the right to life, and now we Americans are witnessing the deaths of about 1.4 million unborn children a year.

In Southern California recently, there was an announcement in the paper about an apartment house owner who instructed his gardener to cut down a tree that had a heron's nest with eggs in it. This property owner found out that it's a violation of the state of California fish and game code to destroy the egg of a bird and was fined $2500 and put on probation. At the same time, across this land we are legally terminating live unborn people inside the wombs of women.

Then, in 1980, with one of the most absurd decisions of the U.S. Supreme Court, we said that we will no longer permit the posting of the Ten Commandments on the walls of the public classrooms of America.

There are many other decisions that could be mentioned, but this gives you an idea of how this philosophy has infected the judiciary. Alan Bloom's book, *The Closing of the American Mind*, talked about how this philosophy has taken over some of the elite colleges and universities of the country where professors are teaching the next generation, who are no longer sure of the existence of moral standards or fixed moral absolutes by which we define and live our lives.

Another elite of this country that has been dominated by this philosophy is television. You may not be familiar with Don Wildmon of the American Family Association. He's one of my heroes in America. He's performing a marvelous ministry by attempting to clean up TV. His volunteer monitors around the country watch programs that exhibit excessive violence, promiscuous sex, or promotion of drugs or alcohol. They contact the sponsors and say, "If you don't clean up who you're sponsoring, we're going to boycott your products."

He's lost some battles, but he's won some. He wrote a book describing his fight in the cultural war of America, called *The Man the Networks Love to Hate*. In this book he describes a survey looking into the background of the 104 top producers in Hollywood. They've produced the programs that we Americans see on the tube day in and day out, week in and week out, *ad nauseam*.

Of these 104 top producers, 45 percent no longer claim to have any religious affiliation whatsoever; 93 percent confess that they seldom or never attended a religious service; 91 percent of them were of the pro-abortion philosophy; 80 percent did not regard homosexual relations as wrong; and 86 percent refused to condemn adultery as wrong. Is it any wonder that men of that background would be producing so much of the program trash that we Americans see on the tube week in and week out, year in and year out?

Vice President Quayle was absolutely right when he made the observation about Murphy Brown giving credence to the idea that childbirth outside of marriage is perfectly normal. These cultural elites have declared war on our values in our society. That's the bad news.

The good news is that there are two institutions in this country that are still dominated by the philosophy of the Judeo-Christian ethic: the church and the family. And Jim Dobson, whom I consider to be one of the premier speakers today interpreting Biblical principles for our lives, talks about this cultural war going on in the country and in these battlegrounds, the church and the family. I think we Americans should take comfort in where the strength of this nation truly is, notwithstanding this assault that's being conducted on our values. Ninety-five percent of us believe in God; 85 percent pause for a moment of prayer, meditation or contemplation each day; and more than one-fourth of Americans say they pray several times a day.

I mention this because the church and the family are the glue that hold our society together. They are our hope for the future because from these two cultural institutions will come the leadership that will provide the foundation for the next century to ensure that we Americans will continue to be the land of the free and the home of the brave.

Some of our critics have a tendency to say: "Well, Dannemeyer, aren't you really mixing religion and the state or religion and government in violation of the First Amendment?" There's a separation of church and state. I believe that separation came from a U.S. Supreme Court decision in 1947 that was without precedent in the law, but is still talked about today.

And I want to make very clear, so that we understand where we are today, that in America it is not the business of any level of government what religion we pursue. That simply is what our Founding Fathers meant by religious freedom. But what is the business of men and women in this country who have religious convictions is that religion and morality are to influence the government, because that's what our Founding Fathers intended.

George Washington said it is impossible to rightly govern without God and the Bible. John Adams, the second president of the United States, said statesmen may plan and speculate for liberty, but it is religion or morality alone which can establish the principles upon which freedom can securely stand. That was what our Founding Fathers gave us.

What about the Congress of the United States of today? What are they doing with the stewardship of power? This member from California in 1991 made a motion to restrict the funding of federal tax dollars for the National Endowment for the Arts to preclude the use or the production of pornographic trash, and guess what happened? A member from the Democratic Party stood up, a Democrat from South Carolina, and moved to table my motion to instruct conferees. There should have been more than 136 of those 435 members of the Congress who voted against that motion to table, in effect voting for that motion to instruct.

Then my colleague from Illinois, Phil Crane, made a motion several months ago to terminate all funding for the NEA, not just to restrict the funding for the production of pornographic material. Only 85 members of Congress were able to search their conscience and find that we should cut out all funding for the NEA. That to me is a very sad, tragic example of irresponsibility on the part of the Congress of the United States.

We in California are up to our eyeballs in the fight as to whether we're going to redefine the family unit so that homosexuality is an alternative life style that will be accepted on a par with the heterosexual life style.

In the Congress of the United States, believe it or not, there are 108 members of the House today— 102 Democrats and six Republicans—who want to amend the 1964 Civil Rights Act to make sexual preference an enforceable federal civil right. That number has doubled; in the 101st Congress there were about half that number. The numbers are accelerating.

In case you haven't noticed, the Congress as it is organized today, particularly the House where I serve, is totally out of touch with the people of this country. It's time for the American public to bring to those serving in the House and the Senate who are irresponsible with other people's money, the retirement they so richly deserve.

You may ask, "Congressman, how do you know who they are? Who can we believe any more? The Democrats blame the Republicans; the Congress blames the White House; the House blames the Senate and so on, and we just don't know who to believe or who to trust." That's a legitimate inquiry, up to a point, but there is an organization called the National Taxpayers Union in Washington, D.C., that annually rates us all on spending and taxing issues. It's a very elite organization, by the way; you must have 15 of those Federal Reserve Notes to join it.

You can get their publication. They analyze the voting record of all members, Democrat and Republican—even the one Socialist from Vermont, Bernie Sanders. About 150 of the 435 House members are big spenders. They've never met a federal spending program they didn't like. They've never met a tax increase they didn't want to embrace. I have a list of 19 from my home state of California who fit into that category. One of them, by the name of Barbara Boxer, is running for the U.S. Senate from California.

This political party is organized on the premise that the two major parties have failed to address some of the most pressing problems in the country. I've shared with you in this cultural war that how we educate the next generation is crucial in terms of assuring the survival of liberty.

We saw in the beginning of the eighties Jerry Falwell, a distinguished religious leader in America, talk about the Moral Majority and the leadership it brought to this country. Jerry Falwell did a tremendous job of organizing the Moral Majority to make political change in America. It was good as far as it went, but what's needed today is a recognition of something that Tip O'Neill said. I didn't agree with the former Speaker from Massachusetts about many things, but he said that all politics is local, and I agree with that. If we want to change America, we need to change who represents us in city councils, in school boards and state legislative races, in boards of supervisors around this country—because who shows up on a school board today may show up in the Congress of the United States ten years from now.

In California, we have embarked on a real effort to elect men and women at the local districts, county central committees of our state, who affirm the Judeo-Christian ethic as a cornerstone of their lives, the cornerstone of the American experiment in self-government.

Only in so doing do we have a chance of restoring to the people of the world the vision that we Americans started with 200 years ago, when we forged that basic document stating that all men are created equal, endowed by their Creator with certain inalienable rights, among which are life, liberty, and the pursuit of happiness.

I want to congratulate Howard Phillips for the courage and vision he's shown for America, for putting the nudge into the political parties that dominate American politics and saying there is a new movement available here for those who want a new way.

And we should not underestimate the seriousness of the task on which we have embarked, because it took John Dewey and his disciples about 50 years to mess up America. The church and the family are the cornerstones from which will come the men and women to do the job of the future.

4. BUSHWHACKED

George Grant

S omething funny happened to the pro-family, pro-life movement on the way to victory. We were Bushwhacked. Just when
everyone was telling us that, after twelve years of
Republican judicial appointments, after twelve
years of Republican vetoes, after twelve years of
Republican leadership, we were on the verge of seeing the scourge of Roe's child-killing provisions
struck down, we were Bushwhacked.

Just when the common wisdom of our day whis-
pered in pious earnest tones that the Supreme Court
was beginning to show "telltale signs of epistemo-
logical self-consciousness," we were Bushwhacked.
Just when the yammering cohorts of the save-the-
starving-third-world-lesbian-co-dependent-whales
lobby in my town and in yours seemed destined to go
the way of dinosaurs, platform shoes, and Michael
Dukakis, suddenly we were Bushwhacked.

We were Bushwhacked. It happened when we
least suspected it. It happened when we weren't
looking. We should have known better.

We should have known better, because we know that, aside from Howard Phillips, just about the only people in Washington today who have convictions are out on parole.

We should have known better when the Republicans told us that they wanted our money, our manpower, our mailing lists, but we could keep our ideas to ourselves. We should have known that there is no strategic advantage in fighting a wolf in *sheep's* clothing over a wolf in *wolf's* clothing. George Bush said "read my lips" when it came to taxes. He said "read my *flips*" when it came to family values. We should have known better on both counts.

Death and taxes. It seems that the Bush administration is taking to heart the old quip about them being inescapable. And, in a brilliant stroke of New World Order consolidation, it has made them one. As a result, the pro-family and pro-life movements, like the country at large, have been Bushwhacked. But then, it's been a long time in coming.

For years it has been the standard practice of the government to pour millions of dollars into the abortion and family-planning industries, draconian programs, in a purported attempt to hold down the burgeoning costs of welfare dependency. Industry lobbyists have argued that, without a comprehensive, nationwide, tax-funded abortion and birth control network, thousands, if not millions, of young girls and struggling mothers and families would be abandoned to an irrevocable spiral of poverty. They would become a strain and drain on the system. Every dollar invested in family planning, they argued, would save two to three dollars in health and welfare costs. Their line of reasoning that you have to spend money in order to save money sounds logical enough to the wooly-minded wonks and dialectical immaterialists inside the beltway. So anxious to demonstrate an odd sort of fiscal responsibility heretofore inimicable to their nature, they have authorized several well-heeled family-planning measures through the years.

In 1964 the Economic Opportunity Act was passed, which included a number of birth control, maternal health, and hygiene provisions. In 1968 the Center for Population Research was established in order to coordinate federal activities in population-related matters. A significant appropriations commitment was passed at that time to provide for contraceptive and abortifacient research, placement, and service.

Then, in 1970 President Richard Nixon, at the behest of his good friend Congressman George Bush of Texas, signed into law the Tydings Act, consolidating the funding base for the Center and granting service contracts and subsidy support for independent providers. The bill created Title X of the Public Health Service Act and set funding precedents for Title V, Title VI, Title IXX, and Title XX, and a whole host of other family-planning, social welfare spending programs that came along in later years.

Now, Section 1008 of the Tydings legislation— which was passed as a rider despite the resistance of its initial sponsors, including young, brave Congressman Bush—stipulated that none of the funds appropriated under the title should be used in programs where abortion was a method of family planning. But then, when have such trivial matters as the law ever really mattered to liberals with an agenda or career politicians with tenure and seniority? Industry giants such as the National Abortion Federation, the National Abortion Rights Action League, and Planned Parenthood quickly discovered that those restrictive provisions were virtually unenforceable and that the government wouldn't try even if they were.

They also discovered, as many others did during that era—a couple of well-heeled, free-wheeling Texans immediately come to mind—that dipping into the deep well of public funding could be phenomenally profitable. The mind-boggling growth of anti-family organizations since the heady days when the Great Society was just being launched is a lesson in how to exploit appropriations for personal and institutional gain, or how to turn the hard-earned tax dollars of the average American into what the Bible calls filthy lucre. We have been Bushwhacked.

Prior to the advent of the Reagan-Bush era, states and organizations that wanted to participate in these various and sundry federal family-planning programs provided by the Tydings legislation and others were required to submit a detailed spending proposal to the Department of Health and

Human Services. Only if and when they could demonstrate legitimate need were funds approved.

In addition, they were obligated to report back to the department on a regular basis on how they spent the funds and how effective those expenditures were. You know, beginner's stuff. It's called accountability.

The Republicans fought those strict accountability requirements on the basis that they were fiscally counter-productive. It argued that the states and organizations were only using these restrictions as an annual excuse to request ever-higher funding levels, which was true.

Providers such as Planned Parenthood would report that they spent $200 million of our hard-earned tax dollars on family planning but that teen pregnancy rose another ten percent. And thus, according to its convoluted logic, more federal funding was needed to combat the teen sexuality crisis.

All of our efforts don't work; everything that we have tried simply doesn't work. Educational programs don't work. When we bring Planned Parenthood into a high school, teen sexual activity rises 51 percent. When we bring a school-based sex clinic into a high school, abortions rise 67 percent. What they say we need is more money. And the administration has said, "Okay."

The solution proposed by the Republicans was to eliminate accountability altogether. The funds would be dispensed with no-strings-attached gifts known as block grants. There would be no federal supervision. No federal control. No federal evaluation. For the first time in its history, Washington wanted to take its hands *off* something. Amazing! There would not even be federal requirements to establish accountability guidelines. The states and organizations would be free to dispense the funds to anyone, rich or poor, for any purpose, however they saw it.

Remember, family-planning programs began as money-saving strategies for the welfare system. In order to save the economy from that money-saving strategy, the Republicans had to devise a new strategy. Deficit conscious, they rushed in to implement the new measures. And in so doing, they gave the abortion industry what was, for all intents and purposes, a blank check.

Now, thoroughly obscured within the belly-folds of Washington's ponderous social services girth, industry leaders have quickly transformed the administration's new money-saving strategy into a tax-dollar black hole. Its metabolism is such that it is constantly in search of new kingdoms to consume. Washington's wonks are only too happy to comply.

In the first two years of the Bush administration, for instance, costs for the family-planning services actually doubled. Maternal and health care funding programs nearly tripled. Social services block grant funding rose from just over two billion dollars to nearly four billion dollars. Population research funding rose 35 percent and community services block grant funding rose approximately 29 percent. Without exception, abortion lobbyists pressed for and won increases in each of their federal tax entitlements.

Thus, with the Republicans, the industry has been able to have its cake and eat it too.

Now program eligibility is determined at the clinic level, by clinic personnel, according to clinic standards, at clinic prices governed by clinic guidelines. That way almost anybody, *anybody* can qualify for the subsidies.

If the clinic operator says you are poor, you're poor. If the clinic operator says you qualify, you qualify. And since Uncle Samuel has to ante up at a premium rate, there are no questions asked, no verification process required, no accountability necessary, no checks, no balances, no rules, no regulations. It's a perfect con game.

Admittedly, the abortion industry's path through bureaucratic Nirvana has not been without its trials, tribulations, and temporary bodhisattvas.

In 1976 the Hyde Amendment was passed. In 1982 the National Eligibility Committee for the combined federal campaign which solicits charitable contributions from federal employees was able to temporarily remove groups such as Planned Parenthood from its list of beneficiaries. In 1983 the Hatch Amendment was introduced. It came within 18 votes of effectively overturning *Roe v. Wade*. In 1984, funding for the international abortion programs in developing countries was temporarily curtailed by the Mexico City Policy. Then in 1986, conservatives nearly ambushed the Planned Parenthood IRS nonprofit exemption status with the Tax

Exemption Equity Act. In 1987, and again in 1990, Title X regulations were temporarily stiffened to exclude any and all programs that performed, counseled for, or referred for abortion, dubbed by opponents as the "gag rule." But each of these efforts, though helpful in pacifying pro-family and pro-life forces, keeping them in the administration's back pocket, have actually proven to be little more than symbolic.

In almost every instance, the pro-abortionists have been able to reverse their setbacks through a masterful use of the courts. They filed innumerable law suits, restraining orders, briefs, tactical delays, and judicial ploys. And as a result, the industry has been able to emerge victorious time after time after time after time. None of the restrictions are currently in place. *None.* So the sad saga continues uninterrupted. A vast proportion of the industry's funding at every level continues to come right out of the American taxpayer's pocket.

In fiscal 1987, Title X funds amounted to a whopping $142.5 million. In 1988 that sum was up to $146 million. During the Bush administration, Title X programs have been augmented with new taxpayer bequests, so that today some $290 million are spent every year. And there are 18 additional federal statutes, as well as hundreds of state and local measures, that authorize public expenditures and support for family planning and abortion programs, policies, and procedures.

Thus, during the family-values, pro-life Bush administration, Planned Parenthood clinics, affiliates, and chapters received annual federal funding under the $19-million Title V provision of the Social Security Maternal and Child Health program. Each year they receive federal funding on the $12-million Medicaid appropriations bill. In addition, those clinics, affiliates, and chapters benefitted each year from the government's $10-million contraceptive development splurge, its $5-million expenditure for contraceptive evaluations projects, its $68-billion spending spree for reproductive sciences, its $16 million on demographic and behavioral research, and it has $29 million budgeted for community services block grants.

We've been Bushwhacked.

Internationally, various Planned Parenthood Agencies have been able to skim the cream off virtually every United States foreign aid package. This includes a lion's share of the more than $200 million in international population assistance funds, the more than $100 million in contraceptive and abortifacient research programs.

The FDA is fighting to keep RU-486, a chemical abortifacient, out of the United States, but you and I paid for its development in the first place through World Health Organization funding. We are fighting ourselves—as it seems we always have.

The fact is that, under the Bush administration, literally billions of dollars have been used to decimate the family and destroy our progeny. That's a lot of money. That's a lot of your money and it's a lot of my money.

We have been scandalously Bushwhacked.

It has been and continues to be a moral and financial scandal that makes Charles Ponzi's famous roaring twenties security sting pale in comparison. With friends like George Bush in the White House, who needs enemies?

If we have to have evil, why should we settle for a *lesser* evil? George Bernard Shaw once quipped that "Chess is a foolish expedient for making idle people believe they are doing something very clever when they are only wasting their time." Bobby Fisher's most recent antics in Belgrade notwithstanding, it appears that Shaw's quip is better suited to pro-family and pro-life Bush supporters than to chess players.

The fact is, we don't have to choose between one candidate who says "Read my *lips*" and another who says "Read my *hips*." We don't have to choose between a candidate who believes that our country needs change to return to the failed policies of the collectivist seventies, versus a candidate who believes that our country needs change to return to the failed policies of the collectivist eighties. We don't have to choose between Tweedle Dum and Tweedle Dee.

I am not supporting Howard Phillips because I want to be a part of a history-making movement—though that certainly has its own unique appeal. I am not supporting Howard Phillips because I am a high-minded opportunist or a starry-eyed idealist. I am not supporting Howard Phillips in an attempt to somehow enhance my reputation with my peers and colleagues. I am not supporting Howard Phillips for a lack of opportunity to participate in the political process of the Republican Party or even the Bush administration.

I am supporting Howard Phillips as a candidate for the presidency of the United States of America because *it's right*. I am supporting Howard Phillips because *he is right*.

No wavering, no waffling, no mumbling, no juggling, no mixed signals, just the truth (see chart on pages 64–65). That's Howard Phillips.

I'm supporting Howard Phillips because his commitment to the sanctity of human life and to the integrity of our republic is not just a preference; it's a conviction. A conviction lived out in his daily life. I'm supporting Howard Phillips because, with him, I know that we won't be Bushwhacked.

In 1912 Theodore Roosevelt saw that the incumbent president was leading the nation to ruin. He saw that his Democratic opponent was a disaster waiting to happen. And so he entered the primaries as a Republican and won them all, handily. When he got to Chicago, he was locked out of the convention. He and all his delegates were left standing in the rain.

So they walked across the street and decided to do something "foolish"—they decided to start a third party challenge to both major party establishments—in Roosevelt's words, "in order that we might somehow save the Republic."

In a moment of brilliant oratory, he stood before the people and he said, "We are few, we have no party apparatus, our resources are nil to none, but we have one thing that shall endure: courage, vision and purpose. We may not win come November," he said, "but we place our mark upon the ages as a testimony to truth. And ever after our children and their children and generations of children to come will know that in times like these, the courageous do not look for the expedient. They take the challenge and they stand."

Therefore, in this day, charged with disintegrating forces, we too must take our stand.

Presidential Candidates: A Pro-Life Evaluation					
Issue	Clinton Democrat	Perot Independent	Bush Republican	Marrou Libertarian	Phillips USTP
Parental Notice	✔	✔	✔	↔	✔
Parental Consent	✔	✔	✔	↔	✔
Planned Parenthood Subsidies	✗	✗	✗	↔	✔
Title V	✔	✗	✗	✔	✔
Title VI	✔	✗	✗	✔	✔
Title X	✗	✗	✗	↔	✔
Title XIX	✔	✗	✗	✔	✔
Title XX	✔	✗	✗	↔	✔
Human Life Amendment	✗	✗	↔	✗	✔
Informed Consent	✔	✔	✔	✔	✔

Issue	Clinton Democrat	Perot Independent	Bush Republican	Marrou Libertarian	Phillips USTP
Gag Rule	✗	✗	✔	↔	✔
Fetal Testing	✗	↔	✔	↔	✔
Vetoes	✗	✗	✔	✗	✔
Valueless Sex Education	✗	✗	✗	↔	✔
State Regulations	✔	↔	✔	✗	✔
UN PF	✗	✔	✗	✔	✔
UN ICEF	✗	✔	✗	✔	✔
World Health Organization	✗	✔	✗	✔	✔
World Bank	✗	✔	✗	✔	✔
Euthanasia	✔	↔	✔	✗	✔
Judicial Appointments	✗	✗	↔	✗	✔
Executive Appointments	✗	✗	↔	✗	✔
Foreign Aid	✗	✔	✗	✔	✔
FOCA	✗	✗	✔	✗	✔
RU-486	✗	✗	✔	✗	✔
% Pro-Life Position/ Record	36%	32%	40%	36%	100%

Key: ✗ = pro-abortion position/record
✔ = pro-life position/record
↔ = no position or conflicting position/record

5. THE STATE OF THE NATION

Otto Scott

Due to what a French author once called "the treason of the intellectuals," most Americans are uninformed regarding the reality of our national situation. This is not due to any lack of intelligence on the part of the people. It is due almost entirely to the lack of honest information. When all the facts are not revealed, it is impossible to come to an accurate conclusion. We are, in other words, a people inundated with propaganda by a press that is intellectually allied with a massive movement that has long since conquered our schools and our bureaucracy.

The people sense this. They know that they are constantly being propagandized. But they are frustrated, because the propaganda is too slick to penetrate. The media operates on the principle that whatever it chooses to print can be verified. But what it does not choose to print cannot easily be discovered. The result is that the people are constantly misled regarding the specifics of our national situation.

We are, therefore, controlled to a far greater extent than is admitted. We are not free. Our exercise of free speech is drastically limited—more limited today than at any time in our national history. We have more taboos, more subjects and groups that are sacrosanct from criticism than our forbears would have believed possible.

We have fewer rights of property than ever before, because even after we pay off our mortgages, we must pay taxes to keep those houses from being confiscated. We are, in that respect, in the same position as the peasants of a bygone Europe living under feudal overlords.

We are taxed without real representation because not only Congress, but *governmental agencies* have the power to tax us, in the name of regulations. These agencies comprise a fourth branch of government, not created by our Constitution, but by Congress with the connivance of our politicized federal judiciary.

Four centuries ago, John Locke wrote about what he called "the delegation of powers." His immediate example was Charles I, who had sent his agents around the realm collecting money from the rich so he could rule without the consent of Commons. Locke argued that no official had the right to delegate the powers of his office to anyone else. One king at a time, he argued, was enough for the realm.

Our Congress is the only body constitutionally authorized to enact laws for the nation. When it created agencies and authorized those agencies to write regulations that have the force of law, it gave to unelected persons outside Congress authority that only Congress is constitutionally entitled to have. In time, Congress not only delegated its own legislative power behind a semantic trick; it also told these agencies that they can hire their own inspectors to monitor regulations. That is a usurpation of the powers of the executive, which is constitutionally charged with enforcing federal laws. Congress also told the agencies they can create their own courts and adjudicate violations of their regulations. That is a usurpation of the judiciary branch, which is constitutionally authorized to rule on the application of federal laws.

In other words, Congress created agencies whose functions combine the three areas deliberately separated by the Constitution. Federal agencies legislate, administrate, and adjudicate. They are answerable only to Congress, which keeps them on an annual leash in the name of appropriations. This means that Congress has not only found a way to circumvent the constitutional separation of powers, but to gather this concentration of power into its own multiple hands.

It means that regulations have been drawn in more detail than is possible in the congressional process. Unelected persons are appointed to *define*, *regulate*, and *adjudicate* all the activities of the nation. This means that we are governed in an immediate, real-life sense, from cradle to grave, by rules drawn by agencies, enforced by agencies and judged, fined, and sometimes jailed through the charges of agencies.

Congress, therefore, rules the nation once removed on a day-to-day basis, much as Charles I extended his tyranny over England through *his* agents.

This congressional end run around the Constitution is anticipated, in practical terms, when the president assumes emergency powers. These set aside *habeas corpus*, the freedom of the press corps, freedom of speech, and other constitutional rights for the duration of the conflict. Executive orders have been repeatedly issued ever since (during both war and peace) and now number over 13,000. These constitute another breach of the Constitution, since they cover areas not constitutionally mandated to the executive whose powers—like those of Congress—are expressly, constitutionally, limited.

The federal judiciary, meanwhile, has been repeatedly charged with exceeding its authority. In this respect, the role of the judiciary is generally misunderstood. In terms of political realities, the courts are largely governed, behind the scenes, by Congress, which controls the judicial system's budget and the bulk of its nominations. The federal courts are often used by Congress to openly enact laws. The independence of the judiciary was effectively destroyed in 1869–70.

Meanwhile, the expansion of federal authority provided state politicians with a model on how to double, triple, quadruple, and quintuple, sextuple and expand their offices, taxes, regulation, and orders over the people in the 50 states. State legislators created state agencies. And the state agencies have added their regulations to the federal regulations. They tax and administrate and judge in the same way as the Feds, along the same lines, and on the same issues, as the federal agencies. Then the counties in each state, as they were created, got into the act. They have boards and commissions and supervisors who issue licenses for businesses, for barbers and construction contractors, and highway firms, and so on. Finally, each city and town and village has its local officials: mayors and deputies and so on. All with the power to tax and regulate, license and supervise, fine and jail.

Nobody has ever put the vaunted scholarly resources of our huge and self-satisfied universities together to make a list—just a list—of all the governments that we have over us, around us, and under us in these United States. No group has ever even counted the number of laws that bind us, like Gulliver, with the myriad strands of regulations. All these laws, regulations, ordinances, statutes, and orders keep mounting, month after month and year after year, until we now have the Clean Air Act, which governs all life in this land. It covers everything that exists, whether animal, vegetable or mineral, whether inert or moving, whether alive or dead. One might call it the God Act, in which the government has decreed it can rule over all creation—in order to recreate the Garden of Eden—even if it kills us.

One is reminded of the *Ancien Regime* in France before the revolution. "France was governed to an extent and with a minuteness hardly comprehensible to anyone not accustomed to a centralized government," wrote one American historian a century ago.

"Hardly a bridge was built or a steeple repaired," he said, "in Burgundy or Provence without a permission signed by the King in Council and countersigned by the secretary of state. The Council of Dispatches exercised disciplinary power over authors, printers and booksellers. It governed schools and revised their rules and regulations. It laid out roads, dredged rivers and built canals. . . . It took general charge of towns and municipal organizations. . . . "

This description is simplified. It summarizes an enormous web of authority that spread between the King and the people, studded with rules, permits and taxes and bureaucrats. Economic historians estimate that taxes took about 50 percent of the total income of all the French people when the revolution started. Our taxes are now estimated to take close to that percentage, in the high 40s.

Many people ascribe this continuing expansion of authority over every aspect of our lives to simple ambition on the part of our political class, which now comprises many millions of individuals whose livelihood comes from being inside the government. This class includes school teachers, who work in the nation's largest single and most corrupt industry. We shall have to exempt the military from these comments, however, because the military is barred from politics as such, and is charged with defending us all from insurrection or attack.

What we can define as the political class is led by professional politicians on federal, state, and local levels who live occupationally and from need, off the federal treasury. They comprise a vast American minority consisting of all races, both sexes and all ethnic backgrounds who have a direct stake in an all-powerful government. Most members of this political class do not think in overall terms. They have no sense whatever as to where their escalating share of our taxes is carrying the nation. They are concerned only with their own careers, or their own day-to-day needs. Their political leaders, meanwhile, are intent only upon increasing the number of their supporters in every possible way.

Governor Clinton calls this "investing in America." He wants to recreate Franklin Roosevelt's New Deal. He wants to launch huge public works programs, to rebuild the physical infrastructure of the land: roads, bridges, dams—and bureaucrats.

One need not wonder who will staff these projects, nor who will be given the management jobs: the Democratic Convention told us who. They will include, in larger percentages than ever before, our official minorities: women, blacks, hispanics, "native" Americans and Asians.

Beyond that, the politicians in both major parties are indirectly telling us that a free people cannot maintain a prosperous nation. Their platforms add up to the proposition that we need more governmental agencies. That we need to increase the political class; that we need the government to provide jobs of last resort, on governmental terms.

That is, of course, the old argument of socialism. First, undermine the private sector. Then legislate it to death. Then say that, since it has failed, the government must step in. And after the government steps in, the government tells us all how to live, and what to do.

What the Democrats tell us directly, the Republicans tell us indirectly. President Bush, accused by the Democrat Socialists of not taking sufficient governmental actions, defends himself by pointing to the Clean Air Act, which places every industry, enterprise and activity under the governmental thumb. Accused of not caring enough for the poor by Democrats who have through the years remarkably increased their ranks, the President points proudly to the latest Quota Bill, which screens the private minorities and closes them against members of the American majority.

If all this were all simply political, we could deal with it fairly directly. Unfortunately the avenues of public expression—the media, music, the theater, the schools—are controlled by American socialists. These do not consist of any single ethnic or racial or even class group, but are spread across the nation. The shorthand description is "intellectuals," though the term is far too flattering. Perhaps we should simply call them the Politically Correct Crowd. They constitute an immense body that masqueraded amongst us in the past as progressives, then liberals in the recent past, and now have the nerve to call themselves moderates.

These are the people who are deliberately changing our language. And it is the new language that is giving us so much trouble. Pat Buchanan is right: we are in a cultural war, and we have to respond in cultural, as well as political terms. This is not going to be easy, because even our dictionaries have become loaded with propagandistic definitions. Words have been unilaterally forced into new uses, and older words have been completely dropped. We are in a situation analogous to that of the ancient Athenians and Spartans, who discovered after 30 years of war that they were speaking different variations of Greek, and could no longer understand one another.

Here in the United States both cultural and political terms have been distorted and misused by our secret socialists in order to misrepresent their critics and to mislead the nation. In the 19th century, for instance, the term "liberal" meant a believer in a limited government. The Politically Correct Crowd, however, believes in an expanded government, but call themselves "liberals." Of course, they do not openly admit that they believe in expanding the government: they simply say that they believe in helping the people, and doing good. Their approach to that goal was succinctly summarized by King James I of England, over 400 years ago. Accused of ruling without respect for the wishes of the people, he said, "I govern not according to the common will, but the common weal."

We are up against people who believe that they are smarter than all the rest of the nation put together. They want to govern *over* us, instead of *with* us. They do not believe in the original American Dream, which was not that every family could own a house of its own (that's a real estate agent's dream). The *real* American Dream was that we could have a government that would be limited by the rights of the people.

That original American Dream is no longer even remembered. And if so noble a concept can be so meanly diminished, imagine how much of our heritage has been brought not only down to earth, but into the mud by those who want to become our cultural, as well as our political masters. They are using our language to change our culture: to misrepresent the natural relations between men and women, to elevate perversity as an 'alternate life style,' to stretch the term 'family' to suit Woody Allen, to call agitators 'activists' and socialists 'moderates.' The list goes on and on. It's our task to puncture these cultural frauds and to do so by using the English language in all its grandeur, by describing people, behavior, and events in their proper terms. It's our task to label intolerance and bigotry for what it is when it spews its hatred against Christianity and white males and the civilization we inherited from Europe.

That's not a simple task, for there's lots to unravel. For instance, the two major parties let loose lots of balloons in New York and Dallas, but they failed to mention the most sinister element of all:

the use of force in the United States, and why the government allows it to continue. Some believe this is simply an accident, but we know better. We know better, because we have seen socialists in other countries encourage the use of force in the same way, for political ends. They did not invent the formula, but they imitated it, beginning at the time of our greatest tragedy to date: the Civil War.

Northern politicians remained silent when the abolitionists used first violent language and then violent resistance over the slavery issue. They knew that silence and lack of a crackdown meant approval, and that it would lead to further violence, and it did. John Brown eventually lit the match by murdering innocent people to make a political point in 1859. War between the states then became inevitable, not because of those murders, but because of their intellectual approval by the North.

The outcome of that war changed our government from a confederation to a unitary state, and spawned the centralized power that bears so heavily upon us today. A watching world was taught, in other words, that the American way of solving a societal problem is through violence in the name of a Good Cause. We were told the Civil War was a great triumph. We were not told that every other nation ended slavery by a stroke of the pen, without losing a life. Ours is a history very narrowly taught.

It may sound as though this excursion into our past is a digression, but it is not. Violence is a subject that is tied directly to governmental power.

Every citizen can agree with Noah Webster that one of our inalienable rights is the right to be physically safe. And it is the duty—one might say the *first* duty of government—to guarantee that safety.

The reason the Civil War was mentioned is because it was allowed to occur in order to expand the power of New England in the form of a central government dominated by New England interests. I mention violence in this nation because it is encouraged by our home-grown socialists, who call themselves moderates and liberals, who hope to channel violence to achieve ultimate power in this land.

Violence is the ladder socialists use to reach power. It is now nearly forgotten, for instance, that socialist arguments fueled the Haymarket Riots and inspired pitched battles between labor and management before World War I. We had bombings. We had the IWW, which proposed to burn wheat fields and set factories on fire to establish what it called workingmen's rights. Those were decades that seethed with socialist discontent, here and in Europe, although living standards were steadily rising, money was stable, and mechanical marvels were being introduced.

We then had the same troubles as Europe, because we are not an island alone in the world. President Garfield was assassinated here at the same time that assassinations became more frequent in Europe. We had the same socialists here that Europe had, only ours called themselves "progressives."

Later, President Wilson talked about "a war to end wars." You can't believe in violent means for good ends any more clearly than that. Nor should it be forgotten that during that war men and women were sent to the penitentiary in this land for criticizing the conduct and goals of that war. American industry was placed under governmental controls for the first time in our history. And American socialists were placed in commanding positions during that war. They learned then that this nation could be governed by decree—and they have never forgotten it. Nor should we.

Historians now believe that World War I injured the modern West as deeply as the ancient Greeks were injured by the 30-year Peloponnesian War. During the period between World Wars I and II, the Socialist Internationale made enormous gains. It was not generally realized that socialism was a single, widespread international movement, because its leaders in various companies used different labels. Changing labels is a socialist skill.

For instance, the Italian editor of a socialist newspaper, Benito Mussolini, called himself a fascist, after the old Italian word for *fasces,* bundled rods that served as a symbol of authority in ancient Rome. He created a socialist system that maintained the facade of capitalism and its inequality of income, its titular ownership of property, but where all real authority was held by the government.

It's ironic to reflect that the term *fascist* today is used by socialists who call themselves liberals or moderates, as a pejorative against conservatives, when fascism, as both a theory and a practice, comes directly from socialism.

Another socialist member of the Internationale was Lenin. He took 50 million gold marks from Germany during a time when his government was at war with Germany, to socialize Russia. But, in true socialist fashion, he changed his party's name first to Bolshevik, then to Communist. Both he and his party were, however, members of the Socialist Internationale for years. And he called the nation he created out of blood and terror the Union of Soviet Socialist Republics. It was based, in true socialist fashion, on governmental control of all private property.

He and his successors launched a series of plans. Five-Year Plans, he called them. Better, no doubt, than Mr. Clinton's Four-Year Plan. It's not necessary to remind you how that socialist experiment worked.

Finally, we saw the rise of a socialist government in post-World War I Germany, called the Weimar Republic. These socialists came to power because President Wilson's socialists believed the German monarchy had to be replaced, and that traditional Germany had to be changed. In a nation defeated in war and scarred by an enormous transfer of wealth from the aristocracy and middle classes to new hands by inflation, the German Socialist Party launched newspapers that promoted abortion on demand, hailed new art that stripped the gingerbread from traditional German architecture in favor of the stark Bauhaus buildings now inflicted upon us, that praised abstract expressionism in painting and formlessness in music and

dance and licentiousness in the theater, and wel-
comed a remarkable eruption of homosexuality and
lesbianism—and vociferous anti-Christianity.

Weimar anti-Christianity did not reach the
depths of the USSR, where priests and nuns were
murdered, churches sacked and cathedrals turned
into anti-Christian 'museums.' But the German Socialists did denigrate Christianity into a distinctly
unfashionable, second-rate intellectual status.

All this spawned an increasingly coarse, almost
obscene level of political discourse, a remarkable
rise in crime, and a successive loss of respect for
government and laws. Politics became polarized
and increasingly partisan. Political parties began to
use thugs to break up one another's rallies. In time
the thugs increased into gangs. And in due course,
the gangs were organized into party armies.

One of these was Hitler's army of "storm troop-
ers," who carried the banners of National Socialism.
Another was the International Socialists, who called
themselves Communists. To forget the role of the
International Socialists in Germany is to misdirect
students of the period and to misunderstand that
contending socialists destroyed Germany. It is also
to overlook the fact that, if the International Socialists had won that contest for control, it is possible
that Germany would have won World War II, because the International Socialists of Britain, France,
and the U.S. would have undermined all efforts
against it.

None of this is being recited simply to say that
socialism injured Russia and Germany. It is cited

because, in each of these nations, socialist governments used selected minorities to achieve specific political power. In Germany, the socialist government of Hitler organized the majority against a single minority. In the USSR, Lenin and company used the minorities as instruments against the Russian majority. In both instances, racial or ethnic differences were deliberately exacerbated for political ends, described as necessary change in the name of justice.

The Germans were told that their loss in war was due to a behind-the-scenes betrayal, and that their sufferings under inflation were the fault of a minority. In Russia the Poles were promised their freedom from the Czarist regime; the Georgians were told they could regain independence, the Armenians that they would be protected from the Turks, the Jews that all discrimination would be ended.

We should, therefore, pay attention when we hear socialist arguments centering on our two largest minorities: blacks and hispanics. Together these minorities add up to nearly 26 percent of our official, statistical population; in reality, they represent even more. This means over 60 million people. They are fed daily a diet of grievances. They are constantly told that their troubles are caused by the American majority. Some hispanic leaders talk openly about the time when hispanics will be the majority in California, New Mexico, Arizona and Texas—and when this entire region will be returned to Mexico. The black youths in the inner cities are told that their income inequality is not due to lack of skills, but to injustices that must be instantly redressed.

Instantly. Not in time, not by work, not by their own efforts, but by the policies of Change set by the government. No other possibilities are mentioned.

The arguments that agitate the black community have grown familiar throughout the nation. We hear them every day. If they riot, it is explained as justifiable Rage. *Hate Whitey* is not simply graffiti: it is a looming reality that makes every inner city unsafe for nonblacks. Our inner cities have become enclaves where majority rules do not apply.

Our government is, of course, aware of this. Congress recently came within a hair of passing a new Crime Act in which 13 new death penalties were to be enforced. Unfortunately, all were in protection of governmental officials. The safety of ordinary citizens does not deserve such a high priority. Yet we endure 23,000 murders a year. Robberies, burglaries and physical assaults are now so numerous that the police are overwhelmed.

These are not only signs of troubles at hand, but of worse troubles to come. When the highest officials in the land are relatively silent about crimes on the scale of the L.A. riots, we are reminded of the silence of Northern officials when the abolitionists got out of hand. As an expert on pre-revolutionary periods, I can assure you that our situation today fits precisely into the patterns that developed in Germany and Russia.

The assault on traditional art, which has reached the level of governmental sponsorship of anti-Christian filth, the assault on harmony and melody and traditional music, the rise of rock bands that use the heavy metal drumbeats of pagan shamans, the jeering cinema dumping on all our values—there's no need to continue. We know the majority culture is under attack. We know the cultural war is real. We know that the minorities are not being organized against the majority for no purpose. We know that intolerance is preached in the name of tolerance, hatred in the name of anti-hatred, racism in the name of anti-racism, censorship in the name of free speech. Orwell would recognize the process: Newspeak is driving out Oldspeak, New Language for Old—and new goals are being mounted in the name of Change.

Some politicians know this. Certainly our socialists, who use an entire lexicon of deceptive names for themselves, know it. What the people do not know is that socialism did not die with Hitler and Mussolini—or Gorbachev and Yeltsin.

Socialism is a full-fledged ideology that permeates the governing classes of the United States, Britain, France, contemporary Italy, and most of the world. The premises of socialism undergird environmentalism. The names change, but the game remains the same.

It is our task to convince people that there is no such system as *voluntary* socialism. In its complete form—and socialists will never be satisfied with anything less—socialism can only be imposed by force. It consists of expanding the government and shrinking the individual. It does not promise to make people rich: it promises not to allow anyone to get rich. It promises the equality of all—on the lowest level of poverty.

It is our belief that the socialists of this land, entrenched though they seem to be in the media, in academe, in cultural circles, and in government, have led us into near crisis and will lead us into a full-fledged crisis within this decade.

History, however, records that those who are capable of perceiving the real causes of a crisis are capable of resolving it. The fact that we are in crisis is indisputable. The primary campaigns of both major parties revealed that a third of their own registered voters failed to support the party leaders or platforms. Pat Buchanan received a good third of all Republican primary votes. The same percentage was achieved in the Democrat Party by Jerry Brown. When Ross Perot, the change candidate, appeared, a third of the voters of both parties turned to him, although he appeared as a mystery without a platform.

No greater proof of national political disillusion could have appeared. In New York, where the Democrat primary was headlined for weeks, only 5 percent of the registered voters cast a ballot. Overall, most Americans no longer see any reason to vote at all. For one thing, all candidates run on one platform and govern on another. For another, nothing seems to change—although, as we have just traced, this is a skilful illusion. Finally, elections no longer settle issues. Campaigns extend around the year, every year.

In reality, disillusion is encouraged. Behind the facade of two major parties who pretend a difference that does not exist, the stage is being set for total control.

Just over the horizon, however, there are signs—ignored by the media—of a long-delayed backlash. We are a patient and tolerant people, but we cannot be fooled forever. The socialist effort to suppress the majority in the name of the minorities will not succeed. It will not succeed because the real American majority consists not of a single race or ethnic group, but of all those who share a belief in, and a longing for the restoration of, the original American Dream of a nation whose government is limited by the rights of the people.

It is that majority that we are gathered to rally. We believe in a party that does not seek to use minorities as instruments against the majority, but a party that represents all who are hard-working, patriotic, and loyal to the traditions of this nation. These are the real Americans, and we welcome them all, irrespective of creed, color, and national origin.

We welcome them, and urge them to join a party led by a man whose courage is high enough to stand tall against a masked elite which claims to be moderate when it is actually radically socialist. A man experienced in the intricacies of government, who has been tested by authority, who has organized this alternative party by his own efforts from the ground up, who is willing to bear the enormous burdens of a third party despite the scorn and silence of the media, the indifference of the threatened, and the fears of the timid.

That man is, as I am sure you know, Howard Phillips, chairman of The Conservative Caucus, fighter against international socialism in the seventies and eighties, political leader *par excellence*. Howard Phillips is the man to whom this nation will turn in the most perilous period of its history.

This is the man whom destiny will discover waiting and ready when the Big Crunch comes, when the meaning of authoritarian socialism will appear in all its greed for power. It is then, later in this decade, that Howard Phillips will be found prepared and ready to take the helm of this newly-born U.S. Taxpayers Party, to move this party from its modest birthplace to a far larger and more important place on the political and cultural landscape of this nation.

6. SOMETHING THAT WORKS

Emmanuel McLittle

I'm not an African-American; I am an American. The ethnic division that plagues our nation is a lie. And yet, it has saturated the very fabric of our culture.

I wondered, as I struggled the last two or three years to get my magazine, *Destiny*, off the ground, why I was having so much trouble, why I was even doing this, why I would possibly go through school as a psychologist to become an editor.

And then I learned a secret that simply knocked me off my bed. I learned that most people, especially baby boomers, are brainwashed from the very moment TV made its debut, from the very moment that we begin to learn about principles. They begin to teach it to us as two- and three-year-old children, in the personages of Mickey Mouse, Bullwinkle, and all kinds of other characters that our parents allowed us to watch because they didn't have the ability to perceive the messages behind them.

Long ago, they started teaching baby boomer children that the personality of human beings could be contained in animals. What was Mickey Mouse if he wasn't just a rat? How could he espouse principles that originated with a God much greater than animals? What we ignorantly did, and didn't know we were doing, was to accept the notion of evolutionists that the personality and the intuitive abilities of human beings could be contained in a mouse, a frog. Today, it's Ninja Turtles; but this didn't happen today, this didn't happen a few months ago. It happened when you and I, many of us, were children, so it is foolish of us to believe that we're going to make Howard Phillips sit at the place he ought to be if you and I don't understand the mechanics of what has happened. We must understand the mechanics, and why liberalism is so successful.

What I have to be grateful for is that, throughout my entire life, something greater than I, smarter than I, was training me to understand why this convention isn't full of people who ache for a leader, as the media has already confirmed to us. They ache for a leader; they are tired of liberalism—even liberals are tired of liberalism.

There is a little jump inside the mind. The perception allows one individual to share understanding with another individual. What liberals have done better than all of us conservatives is to have mastered the ability to make language, even lies, look like the truth. Now we have a liberal by the name of Bill Clinton, a Marxist devil, and a liberal by the name of George Bush running for office, and we have their partners in crime, the media, trying to persuade us that they're on opposite sides of the fence. Because we've lost long ago this ability to perceive.

No one had to tell me that Howard Phillips was the answer to what ails America. I didn't need millions of people to write me letters to say it. I *perceived* that this man spoke and thought the way I did. I've never met him. How could he have my thoughts in his head? It's because what we perceive comes from a greater mind than you and I, and it does not matter whether this mind is in Virginia or Michigan, California or New York. Almost electrical, transmitted in thought. Not in words, but in a wordless way. You and I can clap and give all of the accolades to Howard Phillips that we want to. For me as a black man, that isn't good enough. I also want to get behind something that *works*.

There is a huge lie that we must defeat. You and I have to defeat the idea that many people are more like robots, and you can feed them information that makes them react one way or you can feed that same group of people a *different* set of information and they will react a *different* way, and you can see that they have no other source of knowledge except what they're told. They don't have it inside of them to know.

I'm reminded of the fascinating story that I read in the Scriptures of a day when Jesus and a bunch of His friends were standing around talking, and

He asked what seemed to be a very off-the-cuff question.

He said: "Who do the people think that I am?"

A bunch of answers came. Somebody said, "They think You're Moses or Abraham come back to life."

One of them stepped forward and said, "I perceive that You are the Son of the Living God."

As a psychologist, I was struck that Jesus would turn around and praise this one. The others got their information from people in the streets. This one got his information from something very still and small, and he didn't need it from the outside—a something that spoke to his mind and heart without a voice. You have to have faith to hear and understand something that nobody else confirms. If you have to have it confirmed, you ain't got it.

So when somebody stepped forward and said to Him, "I perceive that You are the Son of the Living God," He knew that this man stood in front of many people in that crowd and said something very different from what everybody else said and risked looking like a fool saying it.

I'm asking you to be more than supporters, to be more than pushers of Howard Phillips' name. You and I have to find a way and a *language*. I am doing it in the black community, creating a magazine that will rebut the roadblocks that have been built consciously and precisely by Marxist psychologists who know how to make black Americans hate the very country that has propelled us to a state of wealth and well-being farther than any other place on the globe.

How do you do that, if not by language? How do you make black Americans hate the place that has fed us, hate the place that has developed us from slaves? We are told that we became slaves when we came to America. The truth is that we *came* from slavery. It was fascinating to learn that the Creator has saved more than just Israel from the Egyptians. He saved Africans *from Africans*, and He saved Swedish people, and He saved Italians. What we saw 3,500 years ago at that trek through the water and through the wilderness was simply a prototype of what He would do again and again. But, He didn't have to open the Atlantic Ocean to let us walk across. He used ships, somebody else's ships.

This is a very difficult concept to understand: how in 300 or 400 years we can come from barefoot, ignorant, disease-ridden slavery and, in some places of Africa from cannibalism, to today being the managers of some of the largest cities in the world. We are among some of the wealthiest people in the world. We have athletes who earn $15 million a year. I can't even *count* to 15 million.

How did we get here? How are we able to accomplish all of these things? And even a deeper question than that: How is it that liberals, who have engineered most of our problems, are able to persuade us to vote and look toward a person like Bill Clinton, who is the bearer of more suffering, more tax dollars being stolen from you and me, although he claims to want to tax the rich? He's going to put another nail in our coffin.

I am not satisfied with simply holding a sign in support of Howard Phillips. There's work to be done to get this man to be taken seriously by the media, by black people. Black people would love to find a real solution to teen pregnancy and the authorization for teens to abort their children— 400,000 last year *without parental consent*.

A study was recently done in Baltimore, Maryland, where, out of 14,000 people arrested for drugs in 1991, 11,000 were black men. My protractors tell me that the reason is racism. In reality, its because they don't want to admit that the programs of the last 30 years backfired and, instead of helping, have virtually destroyed an entire race.

You don't see people wondering and asking for leaders in the Japanese community. They don't need a leader. They're independent individuals. And there are no leaders in the Jewish community. And who is the leader of whites? So can you see the magnitude of my insult when I hear Dan Rather tell me that people like Ice T and Sister Souljah speak for me?

Whites would never allow Madonna to stand as a spokesperson for their group, and I tell black people that we have looked at the wrong group when we try to decide who's holding us back. We have been trained and oriented to believe that conservatism is an enemy of black Americans, and I say that the conservatism of Howard Phillips is our best friend. I want to suggest that you do not become disillusioned with this community that is being led by fools like Jesse Jackson and Maxine Waters. Reverend Jesse Jackson had the audacity to stand in front of 20 million people and compare the pregnancy of Mary to the illicit sexual activity of today. Mary was not homeless, Mr. Jackson, nor was she an unwed mother, nor was she pregnant because she ran around in the streets with government-handed-out condoms that didn't work. This man is supposed to represent spirituality to the black race. Can you not see why we are confused?

Not many of us perceived the cleverness in his comparison at the Democratic National Convention of Mary to today's unwed mothers. If you saw the ovation, if you look at the people that stood up, if you look at the tears in the audience, could you not see people totally fooled, totally unaware of what was happening, totally ignorant of Mr. Jackson's true intent? Millions of black people want what you want, who have never had a language. They're not just trapped in ghettos. They're trapped inside their minds, and they cannot get out. They're still slaves.

From Dan Rather to Jesse Jackson to the NAACP to the Urban League, leaders have told black Americans from childhood to be liberals, except they don't know it. If you were in South Africa and you were trained in the way that they train people in South Africa, you would do something because you had been trained to do it that way. And black Americans think the way they do because of training that begins at birth. It is in our churches, in our gyms, in our schools; it is everywhere we go. There is a notion that white America owes black America, and that America is racist, and that there is no love for America in black America. I want to rebut it. On the pages of a magazine called *Destiny*, one of the first things I wrote is that I am a black man and I love America. I don't *want* it to be changing, and I have been gifted with the perception that it *is* changing. Liberals are so clever, though, that they dare not do it quickly. They're doing it very slowly.

Over a period of 30 years, I can no longer recognize the America that we live in. It has changed. Homosexuals have a special place in this world now that they didn't 30 years ago. It was not possible 30 years ago for a 14-year-old girl to become pregnant and actually be praised for it. It was not possible for celebrities to be pointed to as leaders and spokesmen if they stood on stages and talked in the most negative and dirty way about the body of a woman. The hypocrisy of feminists who allow that, and who do not allow a man to have any say in what happens to his unborn child!

Several thousand years ago, Jerusalem was in a state similar to where America is headed. The Soviets of that world were called the Roman Army, the Roman Empire. It was spreading itself all over the globe. Jerusalem was simply one of its testaments.

And so there was a government that took over, because conservatism wasn't what it ought to have been back then. It took Jerusalem over, and there was a man like Howard Phillips that did nothing but speak common-sense truth to people. You might think that He walked around talking about God all the time, but He also talked about politics.

There was another man running around doing the same thing, a modern-day Jesse Jackson. They called him Barabbas. Fate would have it that these two men would occupy the same stage at the same time. There were no microphones. In fact, it was a trial, because the governor at that time knew that there was something wrong with the conviction of Jesus. He gave people a chance to choose, sort of a makeshift election.

And he held his hand over the head of Jesus and said, "Will you choose this Man to enjoy release from His sentence of death, or do you choose the other?"

Lo and behold, all of those people—save for a handful—chose the politically correct Barabbas. They didn't understand, they could not perceive, and the conservatism in that day was weak.

Understand that this story was written to show us a principle which does not does get old. Who will you choose? You and I are scattered among a crowd of 250 million people who are going to choose in this election and the next. The characters have changed, and today we have Howard Phillips, whom the media hardly recognizes; Bush, whom the media pretends to hate; and Clinton, their pretty boy. And we're being given a *choice*.

I want to be associated with something that *works*, and I am not interested in seeing Howard Phillips as fodder for liberal media personalities to laugh at. I want a ticket to the swearing-in ceremony in '96 or four years afterwards.

And so there is work to do. First we must define this new conservatism, and it must be a clear, definite, and sharp conservatism of common-sense wisdom. It isn't in vogue, but neither was liberalism at one time, so it is possible that you and I can learn it. Jesus said: "You can be as wise as serpents." You've got to go out and read about serpents. You've got to read how this animal can sit on a tree for two days and actually become the color of the bark so that his enemy doesn't know he's there. We can *learn* it.

You and I are going to have to grasp that same wisdom to be as wise as a serpent, but not with the intent of hurting anybody. Like a dove, gentle, because we realize that our fellow man is being controlled by marketing and packaging techniques that are far more advanced than most of us can understand. The members of the media have so mastered language that they tap right into your brain in a 60-second commercial and make you go out and buy something.

They do it skillfully. Now, let's get smart. We want to win. If America falls, where will we go? Over two million people on the continent of Africa are infected with AIDS. Europe is a mirror of the Soviet Union. Italy isn't big enough for us. Switzerland is too cold.

Where will we go? Where will we go if our continent, if this bastion, this macro-cosmic duplicate of paradise falls? Where will we go?

I don't know about you, but I have problems paying my taxes on my home now. I don't want to pay 30 percent somewhere else. I'm serious about staying here, and I know what it's going to take—a Howard Phillips and his brand of new conservatism.

I want what I have said to you to be a seed for some of you who have made enough money already to cut back, go part-time, and work part-time for Howard Phillips to move him from the back shelf to being seriously considered.

You've all seen his literature. Have you seen anything else that makes any more sense? Don't make the mistakes of present-day conservatives. They're just conservatives in their *heads*. I'm a conservative in my *heart*. I'm a conservative after nine o'clock at night as well as before nine o'clock in the morning. I'm a conservative all the time. I'm a conservative with my wife. I'm a conservative with my children. I'm a conservative in my heart, sitting on the train all by myself.

I adjure you: don't be the same old kind of conservative who has caused nearly all of the modern generation to hate conservatism. They can see that it's phony. They can perceive that there is no difference between George Bush and Bill Clinton. But we give them a candidate that is a sharp, clear, difference, who cannot be labeled as racist, who cannot be labeled as far-right radical. Howard Phillips makes sense. We can make America work again—for us all.

7. HONEST MONEY

Dr. Edwin Vieira

*T*he problem with our country is twofold. On the one hand, we are buried beneath a mound of popular ignorance. On the other hand, we are assaulted by an impenetrable hubris.

I still travel around the country and give talks to people, sometimes in relationship to a court case I have because I'm an attorney. I get to the hotel, and the first thing they ask me when I register is: "How do you intend to pay for this?" And I will say, "Do you take Federal Reserve Notes?" The answer in 95 percent of the cases is: "No, we take American Express, Visa, or MasterCard."

And the other five percent—the young person behind the counter, usually a management trainee out of junior college—will say: "Well, I don't know, let me ask the manager." And he'll come back and say: "No, we take American Express, Visa, and MasterCard."

And then I'll pull out one of those little green things we all have in our pocket. I'll pull out one with George Washington on it, and I'll point to the legend on the top: "Federal Reserve Note." And we all laugh.

But it isn't funny. They don't know what their own money is.

On the other side of the coin is hubris. I read a few of years ago an article stating that the Federal Reserve has a vault in Culpepper, Virginia, supposedly stuffed full of Federal Reserve Notes. It is bomb-proof, in anticipation of nuclear war.

These people are so imbued with their own arrogance and the sin of pride, that they actually think that, after a nuclear war, people will take Federal Reserve Notes!

The only thing that's more ridiculous than that is the plan that the IRS has for collecting income taxes after a nuclear war. And there *is* such a plan.

We have an economic problem. Trillions and trillions of nominal dollars, of unpayable debt. This debt will not be paid. The machine has clearly malfunctioned.

What do you do when a machine malfunctions? You consult the owner's manual. You go back to the set of instructions and see what went wrong.

In this particular case, the set of instructions is the Constitution of the United States. These problems are not new; they were faced by the Founding Fathers of this country in the late 1700s, and in 1787 when the Constitution was written, the Founding Fathers were concerned precisely with the problem that faces us today: the role of government in the nation's monetary and banking systems.

They themselves had been eyewitnesses to a raging inflation followed by a business depression that was precisely the result of the emissions of bills of credit—paper money—by both the Continental Congress and the various states in the War of Independence.

And it was as a result of that experience that they very carefully drafted the monetary powers of the Constitution, precisely to prevent repetition of such a calamity, by outlawing what James Madison in the *Federalist Papers* called "the fallacious medium and the improper and wicked project of paper money."

Let's review some of those provisions in the operator's manual. Article I, Section 8, clause 5.

The Constitution clearly adopts silver and gold coin exclusively as the money of the United States. The standard of value in this monetary system is the dollar. The Constitution uses that word twice: "the dollar."

What was a dollar in 1787? Was it one of these green pieces of paper? If you had taken every coin and bill of credit that had ever been created in the history of the world and laid it on the table in front of the Founding Fathers of the United States, every one of them would have picked up one particular coin if you had asked them what a dollar was.

It was a silver coin containing $371\frac{1}{4}$ grains of silver.

The Constitution provided in those two provisions that the legal value of all silver coins must be proportional to that weight of silver they contain in comparison to the dollar. And the legal value of all gold coins would be proportional to the weight of gold they contain in comparison to the dollar at the prevailing market exchange ratio between gold and silver.

Article I, Section 8, Clause 2 and Article I, Section 10, Clause 1: The Constitution clearly prohibits the emissions of any form of paper money—what the Founding Fathers called "bills of credit." No state shall emit bills of credit. And the latter provision disables the states from imposing on unwilling creditors anything but gold and silver coins as tender in payment of debts.

If only gold and silver coins can be tender of payment of debts, then it would be fairly clear that only gold and silver coins could be the official governmental money of the United States.

In Article I, Section 8, Clauses 1, 2, and 5, and Article I, Section 10, Clause 1, and the 5th, 9th, 10th, and 14th Amendments, the Constitution declares that Congress and the states may not levy forced loans on the people, may not seize the peoples' gold and silver except through proper taxation—and may not prevent the specific performance of private contracts that explicitly require payment in silver, gold or other monetary media.

That's clear enough on the face of the document. So what has gone wrong? It's very simple. The people who have been in control of the mechanism have not followed the rules.

Historically, we go back to February 1862—the first time Congress ever emitted legal tender paper currency, the so called "greenbacks" of the Civil War. That was the beginning—the first time since 1787 that anyone had considered that a legal tender paper currency might be legitimate.

In 1913, Congress created the Federal Reserve system, a semi-private, semi-public banking cartel that asserts a kind of political independence from Congress, from the President, from the courts—and especially from the electorate.

The Federal Reserve is especially privileged to emit its own paper currency—Federal Reserve Notes. And although these notes have been declared by Congress to be obligations of the United States (in complete disregard of Article I, Section 9, Clause 7 of the Constitution), what has happened to this obligation?

Congress has never enacted a single statute authorizing the dollar amount of such obligations that the Federal Reserve creates. There is absolutely no legislative authorization for one piece of all that paper, even though the effect of the generation of this paper has been to take money out of the public treasury. This is especially true now, with the banking collapse, through such mechanisms of the Federal Deposit Insurance Corporation.

In 1933 Congress declared Federal Reserve Notes legal tender. This was the first time they were declared legal tender, under Mr. Roosevelt.

And it rescinded the requirement that those notes be redeemable in gold coins for citizens of the United States—the famous "gold seizure."

In 1933-34, Roosevelt closed the banks and seized the gold coin. Apparently he got only about 40 percent—the people weren't that stupid then. They didn't turn it all in.

He nullified all public and private contracts that called for payment in gold, a so-called repudiation of the gold clauses.

I believe it was Roosevelt's first fireside radio chat just after he closed the banks, days after he'd been inaugurated. He came on radio to tell people what was happening. And he explained to them the fractional reserve banking system. He said, "We have to do this because the banks don't really have all of that gold coin. They can't redeem."

I suggest that if the President of the United States felt it was incumbent upon him to come on radio and tell people what was happening, the fractional reserve system was not very well understood by the people. The fraud wasn't understood then and it certainly is not understood now.

In 1965, Congress terminated the coinage of constitutional silver dollars, and authorized the first debased coinage, so-called "clad coinage," the sandwich coins, mostly copper, with a little nickel washing.

In 1968, Congress terminated redemption of any form of United States money in silver coin. So it was not until 1968 in this country that we actually had a so called "fiat" currency. FIAT—let it be money. It really *isn't* money. Let it *be* money because the government says so.

That was not so long ago—approximately 25 years. And look how quickly the economy has gone down and debt has gone up. This has not been a matter of *centuries;* it's been a matter of *decades.*

In 1985—apparently through the lobbying of Senator Helms, Mr. Ron Paul, and others—Congress authorized the minting of new silver and gold coins, but these coins don't circulate.

Why? Because their face values are completely out of line with their market values. So, since 1968, the money of the United States has consisted essentially of legal tender Federal Reserve Notes which are not redeemable in anything. They're an IOU-nothing currency, as John Exter likes to call it.

Since 1968 the supreme law of the land, the Constitution, certainly hasn't changed. There's been no amendment.

These modern-clad coins contain no silver or gold. All the silver and gold coinage of the country has been withdrawn as the base of the monetary system, even though Article I, Section 10 requires that nothing but gold and silver coins be a tender in payment of debts.

Irredeemable Federal Reserve Notes have become the nation's currency. You'll notice something about irredeemable Federal Reserve Notes. Bills of credit were precisely that: they were bills of credit to be redeemed. Even the greenbacks in the Civil War were eventually redeemed in 1875 with the resumption of *specie* payments.

The current Federal Reserve Notes are notes that promise to pay you *nothing*—they're bills of *discredit.* They're already repudiated before the ink is dry down at the Bureau of Engraving.

The Federal Reserve system is composed of thousands of private banks, and it controls the money supply, interest rates and all the other monetary phenomena, even though the Congress of the United States under the Constitution has sole power to coin money and regulate the value thereof.

To fully comprehend the significance of the Federal Reserve system requires recognition that there is no such thing as politically neutral or politically independent money. Money is both a medium of exchange and a form of property. In fact, it's a method for implementing contracts that transfer property among people.

So even in a free-market economy with a limited government, money exhibits a necessary political character, to the degree that the government protects the monetary system from private fraud and public looting. It reflects the degree to which the government respects and protects private property and the right of private contracts.

A free-market economy has one kind of money; a mixed economy or a fascist economy has another kind of money; a socialist economy has yet another kind. The money always reflects the political values of the system.

What's called the political independence of the Federal Reserve system is a misdirected concept, because the Constitution originally made our money independent of electoral politics. It did that by fixing the unit as the silver dollar, outlawing bills of credit, and allowing only gold and silver coins to be legal tender in payment of debts. That was a political determination because the Constitution is a political charter. It settled on one very specific political formula for money—a money of intrinsic value, the supply of which the political authorities could not manipulate for their own purposes.

That was the goal of the Constitution: to take money out of politics so that it couldn't be used for improper purposes.

The creation of the Federal Reserve system in 1913 didn't make Federal Reserve Notes politically independent or politically neutral; it merely changed the political character of the monetary system by empowering a small unelected clique of self-styled experts to control the supply of Federal Reserve Notes, to control interest rates and to control all the other monetary and banking phenomena.

Thus, as contrasted with the constitutional system, the Federal Reserve system really politicized money, because now it enabled the politicians, the administrators and a few specially selected special-interest groups to exercise the very influence over the country's money and banking systems that the Constitution had disallowed.

In other words, there was a political revolution in 1913.

Americans tend to accept the description of the Federal Reserve as politically independent because the apologists for that system have been very successful over the years in removing money and banking as issues in the political arena. Americans don't hear political parties and political candidates discussing those matters.

Yet, it is of vital political importance that no major political movement or party has advocated until now the immediate restoration of the constitutional monetary system.

It's of vital political importance that no major political movement has demanded that paper currencies be redeemable in silver, gold, or any other commodity.

It's of vital political importance that no major political movement has attacked inherently fraudulent fractional reserve banking. It's of vital political importance that no major political movement has denounced the corrupt relationship between the government and the banking industry to the Federal Reserve, the Federal Deposit Insurance Corporation, and all the rest of those fraudulent agencies.

It's of vital political importance that no major political movement has challenged the government's use of monetary and banking systems to regulate the economy and to impose what essentially amounts to police state surveillance on the financial lives of individuals.

It's of vital political importance that the short-run effects of the Federal Reserve's monetary policies are very unclear to the average American. Identifying who gains, who loses, what's gained, what's lost and why all this happens is very difficult, even for economists and political scientists.

It's of vital political importance that members of Congress have no incentives or strong *dis*incentives to investigate the policies of the Federal Reserve.

And it's of vital political importance that the general public is unable to deal effectively with the Federal Reserve, even as its supposed agency of government.

Obviously a group that can take all of these crucial matters out of the arena of political discourse without complaint from any significant part of the public must be extremely powerful. Precisely how the apologists for the Federal Reserve were successful in stifling political debate on money and banking, the history books don't satisfactorily explain. But it's clear enough that the Federal Reserve system was established to remove the Constitution as the arbiter of monetary policy, and to guarantee instead that a particular special-interest group was monopolistically represented in the determination of that policy, with the peculiar benefit to that special-interest group and its clients.

So, today we have a system of fiat money, unlimited fractional reserve banking organized under a fascist bank cartel. That's precisely what it is. In the most fundamental sense, although his troops lost the war, Mussolini won the war of ideas because the institutions of fascist control are now *our* institutions. And under either Mr. Bush or Mr. Clinton, they will only advance in terms of their power. In this particular system, the Federal Reserve Board plays a very simple role. When public confidence in the monetary and banking system weakens, the

Federal Reserve Board steps in to restore confidence by manipulating interest rates, money supply, or reserve ratio.

It may use drastic means to do so, but it never uses means so drastic that they seriously endanger the long-term interests of the bank cartel, its satellite industries, or its political cronies. They will always save themselves; they will bleed every American dry, but they will save the banking system because that is the focus and source of their power.

The insoluble problem that the Federal Reserve faces, however, is that fractional reserve banking suffers from inherent instability that increases over time, because that base fractional reserve banking is a pyramid scheme. Fractional reserve banking is a confidence game in both senses of the term. The Federal Reserve Board, the banking cartel, and the politicians of the American one-party state operate on the theory that you can fool all the people some of the time, and some of the people all of the time, and that's good enough!

They forget that, as Mr. Lincoln added, you can't fool *all* of the people *all* of the time. Over time, some people, and perhaps even relatively large numbers of people, learn what's going on and they act on that knowledge. So, the remaining lifetime of the Federal Reserve system and its confidence game is probably relatively short. It doesn't follow that its end will be sweet. The real, pernicious significance of this system is not simply monetary in character; it's not simply a control mechanism for a national banking cartel. Ultimately, it's the most important mechanism in a system of fascist economic regulation that's been set up in this country, slowly but surely, since the turn of the century, since President Wilson.

This explains the political independence of the Federal Reserve system in a much more logical way than the notion that money and banking aren't really important political issues. If you're going to have a fascist state that will regulate the economy with relative autonomy from the electoral public, remember: that's what a fascist state does; it runs the system without approval from the victims.

The monetary agency then has to claim political independence, because without political independence, they become responsible, and if they become responsible, there is no fascist system.

What's important, though, is that no constitutional branch of the national government—not the Congress, not the president, and not the ultimately corrupt toadies in the federal judiciary—dispute the Federal Reserve system's supposed independence, which proves that all of these branches have been co-opted as agencies of this fascist state and are all subject to whatever control mechanisms really operate behind the scenes.

What are the major consequences of the Federal Reserve system?

First, the people don't enjoy a form of money that serves as a long-term store of value any more. Instead, they must use as their media of exchange irredeemable Federal Reserve Notes that lack any intrinsic value. Since World War II, they've gone down and down even in exchange value—90 percent of their value has been lost since World War II.

Second, because Federal Reserve Notes lack any intrinsic value, their purchasing power is subject to political manipulation. That is, there's been a reason that it's gone down. It's been *made* to go down.

Third, the emission of intrinsically valueless Federal Reserve Notes is the prime means by which the government operates a system of oppressive hidden taxation to increase the price of goods and services that the public calls "inflation."

Fourth, by operating as a system of hidden taxation, the emission of intrinsically valueless Federal Reserve Notes enables the ruling oligarchy in this country to redistribute the nation's wealth from one group to another.

How much? Since World War II, it has been $6 trillion. The American Institute for Economic Research in Massachusetts does a study every year. How much redistribution of wealth has occurred through inflation? Since World War II, $6 trillion has been redistributed. Attila the Hun never made that much.

Fifth, by functioning as a mechanism for the hidden redistribution of wealth, the emission of intrinsically valueless Federal Reserve Notes systematically corrupts the electoral process.

How? Because it enables the politicians to buy votes with promises of newer expanded government spending programs that are made possible only by the banking system's ability to monetize the public debt.

Sixth, by linking the banking system to the public debt, the Federal Reserve licenses the private banks to loot the public treasury. It does this initially by guaranteeing Federal Reserve Notes as obligations of the United States and making them legal tender so that they circulate—and ultimately by providing bailouts of the bankers to FSLIC, RTC, FDIC, and whatever comes down the pike, when the scheme of inherently fraudulent fractional reserve banking collapses.

Seventh, the Federal Reserve system and its phony paper currency function as the key mechanism of the scheme of fascist central economic planning that misdirects and wastes resources, and thereby lowers the standard of living for the vast mass of Americans for the benefit of the privileged few.

The present system of irredeemable Federal Reserve Notes and fractional reserve banking destabilizes the economy by perpetuating the so-called "boom and bust cycle." Inflationary expansion, followed by recession, followed by increased inflation and so on—and the cycles become wilder and wilder until you finally have a catastrophe.

Some misguided people call this the "business cycle," which is very unfair because accurately it should be labeled the "political money cycle." It's the inevitable effect of manipulation of the supply of money by politicians and the special interest groups that they serve through the Federal Reserve.

What must be done? Cato used to open and close every speech in the Senate of Rome with the phrase: "Carthage must be destroyed!"

That's the answer. The Federal Reserve system must be destroyed!

We can live with the IRS. We may not *like* it, but we can live with it. But economically, in the long run, the Federal Reserve system is a death sentence. We can't live with phony money—no society has lived with phony money.

Every paper money system in the history of the world has gone bust. And if you think we're smarter than every other nation in the history of the world, ask yourself why we have had millions of abortions in the last 20 years.

Think of all the other crazy things this country has done. It's not going to be able to handle a paper money system any better.

Germany in the 1920s was probably the most cultured country in the world, perhaps in the history of the world. Science, art, literature, philosophy, economics, war. It was only because the whole world turned against them that they lost World Wars I and II.

They had an experience with paper money in 1922–23. Read about it if you want to know what happens in hyperinflation.

Another classic example is Argentina, now a basket case. In World War I, it was fifteenth in the world in wealth per capita. Downhill—because of bad political policies and primarily bad monetary and fiscal policies.

Its neighbor, Brazil, is one of the wealthiest countries in the world in terms of resources. A basket case! And look at the United States. Are we following the same route? Are we smarter than the Brazilians and the Argentinians?

Reforms of the type set out in our platform have been successfully implemented twice before in America's history.

The first time was throughout the nation following the War of Independence and the adoption of the Constitution in the late 1700s. They had the same problem we have today. They had the Continental Currency, the state bills of credit; they had business depression; they had rampant inflation, and they had a huge political group demanding repudiation of debts and other kinds of government bailouts. Mr. Clinton would have been considered a moderate in those days.

Fortunately, the people in control of the Constitutional Convention were true conservatives. That's why I fear a Constitutional Convention today. Can you imagine who would chair it? Teddy Kennedy? The conscience of the Senate, as the *Washington Post* calls him.

They took a country that had just been through a major war, was in the throes of economic depression, and was involved in a terrific political battle over even the ratification of the Constitution and unity among the several states, and put together the soundest political money system the world had ever seen.

And it lasted for about 70 years, until the Civil War, until a major crisis.

The second time these reforms had been adopted was following the Civil War in the South.

The South had precisely the same problem, and perhaps worse: it lost the war and was economically prostrate.

It had no currency because the Confederate notes were declared illegal; in fact, to a large extent, they were declared treasonous because they had been used in the prosecution of the rebellion.

They introduced what still existed in the Union—a gold and silver monetary system, and the Supreme Court actually made a few correct decisions as to how that should be implemented in the southern states.

The constitutional reform of the monetary and banking system is not merely a theoretical possibility, a pie-in-the-sky idea. Instead, it is a practical program that could work today if it were implemented, just as it worked in the past.

America really has no choice in the matter. Irredeemable Federal Reserve Notes will remain what Madison rightly called "the fallacious medium and an improper and wicked project," whether Americans act or not.

And the consequences of having a fiat money and fractional reserve banking system will work themselves out, whether Americans like it or not. The chickens will come home to roost. You can hear them clucking outside.

The imminent demise of the Federal Reserve system is not going to be sweetness and light. Something has to be done, and the question is: what will be done? Will the American people wake up and destroy the Federal Reserve system before the

Federal Reserve system destroys the American economy? Or will the American people allow the Federal Reserve system to destroy the American economy and then turn, as people have always turned when monetary systems collapse, to strong-man totalitarian rule?

That's the choice.

This party represents an opportunity—perhaps not in this election, but perhaps by the next one—to begin to convince the American people to take that alternate road.

It will only be the second time in world history it ever happened. What was the first time? The War of Independence, where there was a monetary and banking collapse in the context of total social chaos, out of which came a sound structure, politically and economically.

Look at the German example and see what came out of that—it broke the back of the Weimar Republic, and eventually they came up with Hitler. There was an example of a highly cultured country and they turned into a totalitarian party. There are many other examples throughout history.

We're looking at the hope that the people in this party and the people who join and ally with them in the next few years can essentially do what the Founding Fathers of this country did in the late 1700s.

That is probably the greatest historical challenge that this country has ever faced. It's bigger than either war; it's bigger than the Great Depression. It probably is even bigger than the original difficulties that the country faced in the War of Independence, because the total burden of debt and social problems allied with it are greater.

One can only pray to God that the American people are capable of dealing with this challenge.

8. THE BETRAYAL OF AMERICA

Ambassador David Funderburk

During the Reagan years, conservative groups sprang up all over Washington. Amazingly though, they came to love Washington; they went to the White House; they got on television; they raised a lot of money; and in the end, they betrayed their principles. They did not speak out against taxes; they did not speak out against the rising deficit; they did not oppose George Bush in his aid to Communist governments such as Red China.

But during all of the false and empty rhetoric of the conservative Revolution, there was one honorable man in Washington. His voice was always loud and clear—putting America first, putting conservative principles of less government and fewer taxes first, exposing Communist tyranny and U.S. aid to Communists. That man was Howard Phillips.

We know where Howard Phillips stands. He did what he said he would at the OEO: he cut bureaucracy and they squealed like stuck pigs. He did not compromise himself by seeking favors from the White House. He challenged the Soviet and Romanian Communists head-on during his Baltic tour and his monitoring of the rigged Romanian elections. And he practices what he preaches.

Yes, Bob Dornan, one of the presidential candidates *is* a womanizing draft-dodger. Yes, Pat Buchanan, Clinton & Clinton *don't* share our values and our vision for America. But no, Bob and Pat, now is *not* the time to stand beside the Bush who stands beside Deng Xiaoping, Li Peng, Boris Yeltsin, Eduard Shevardnadze, Serbian boss Milovan Milosevic, Romanian son of Ceausescu, Ion Iliescu—all of these long-time Communists. And now is *not* the time to stand beside the Bush who stands beside the likes of Dick Darman, Larry Eagleburger, David Souter, Bob Mosbacher, Senator Seymour, and the late Armand Hammer. Now is the time to stand beside one who has been true to freedom fighters against the enemies of freedom: Howard Phillips.

Yes, Ronald Reagan, it is time to clean the House, but it's also time to clean the Senate, and it's time to clean the White House. We have had enough of the lesser of two evils. Two ultimate insiders, two ultimate establishment men, two Trilateralists, one-time CFR members, advocates of big government, more socialism, and aid to One-Worlders and socialists around the world.

The George Bush I dealt with as U.S. Ambassador to Romania is one who has consistently appeased and aided Communist tyrants and betrayed American

principles. In George Bush's acceptance speech at
the Republican Convention, he referred to the death
of Communism, but he forgot to mention his long-
time Most-Favored-Nation status and other assistance to the still-Communist mainland Chinese or
to other neo-Communists around the world.

After spending six years in Communist lands, I
knew something was wrong when George Bush
came to Ceausescu's Romania, and when I met him
in the White House and in his office. I knew something was wrong when Lawrence Eagleburger
warned me not to bring up Communist atrocities or
technological transfers. I knew something was
amiss earlier this year when a threatened lawsuit
against me for my book *Betrayal of America: Bush's
Appeasement of Communist Dictators Betrays American
Principles* came, demanding that I "cease and de-
sist" distribution of the book. But this banned book
is still available on the table outside this convention.

When the Chinese Communists rolled tanks into
Beijing and when they instituted martial law, Bush
appeased them by granting Most-Favored-Nation
status eleven days later. Then came the Tiananmen
Square slaughter and the Scowcroft/Eagleburger
trips, sucking up to appease the Butchers of Beijing
with blood on their hands. Bush is still rewarding the
Chinese Communists today, no lesson learned.

When Gorbachev sent tanks and paratroopers
into the Baltic capitals and killed freedom fighters,
Bush appeased Gorbachev with promises of MFN.
Russian troops are still in the Baltics today and they
are still firing on Romanians in Moldova. Bush is

still rewarding Moscow and Yeltsin, no lesson learned.

When I personally briefed Bush on Ceausescu, who killed thousands of innocents, destroyed churches, exported arms and drugs, and assisted international terrorists, Bush appeased Ceausescu by praising him and continuing MFN and U.S. financial assistance. Romanians today still live under a dictatorship led by an old Communist colleague of Ceausescu and Gorbachev. Bush is still rewarding Bucharest, sending a letter August 3, 1992, to the Senate, asking for Most-Favored-Nation status to Romanian so-called neo-Communists, no lesson learned.

When I traveled to Eastern Europe this summer, I saw the same Communists running governments—of course, they were calling themselves something else. The former head of Romania's KGB, or Securitate, just wrote a new manuscript in which he documents that the secret police in all of the old bloc countries, with the exception of the special case of East Germany, are the same characters that he worked with through the past 30 years—still backing old Communist dictators behind the scenes. And the U.S. government, of course, is still funneling money to keep these old Communists in power. When I was there this summer, former religious and political dissidents who were beaten and jailed for their beliefs asked me, again, as always, why FDR sold them out at Yalta. And this year, they asked why George Bush sold them out at Malta. The Communists and socialists are not all dead, regardless of what the news media says in this country. Can anyone be so naive and ignorant of what is really going on as our President and State Department? Or do they have another agenda?

When I tried to report to the United States about aid and technology going to Communist murderers, Larry Eagleburger sent me "eyes-only" cables telling me to back off. After all, they had a cozy relationship with Ceausescu. We know that Eagleburger served as President of Kissinger Associates for over four years, making $1.1 million the last year. We know he was on the board of Yugo America, a Yugoslav Communist company, on the board of LBS Bank, a Yugoslav Communist bank convicted of money laundering, and whose branch, BNL, diverted U.S. loans to arms purchases by Saddam Hussein. We know that Eagleburger, as Deputy Secretary of State under Bush, kept U.S. support going to the Serb Communists to the bitter end. And we know that Eagleburger, Scowcroft, and Kissinger have gotten rich off their connections with Communist bosses, and, in the process, have helped keep the tyrants in power, while those seeking freedom have been crushed and ignored. And now, as his reward, Eagleburger was named in August by Bush as Acting Secretary of State for the rest of Bush's term.

Yes, we believe there are masters of deceit and deception. They have been in Moscow for 75 years, and in New York and Washington for God-knows-how-long. Our constitutional republic is being undermined by those who put money and power and a New World Order ahead of our principles. You know about the national debt—the mortgaging of our children's future. The insanity of government spending, government growth, government debt, and government taxes has got to stop. And we know that the liberal Democrats and the country-club Republicans are not going to stop the growth of socialism in this country.

Communism under the name "Communism" may be dying, but socialism is thriving everywhere—especially here in the United States. The United States is moving closer to adopting socialism than we would imagine. Marx and Lenin advocated, through a public school system, abolition of the family and tradition, in favor of free love. Political correctness is doing a number on tradition in our colleges. And, in schools, ethnocentrism and environmentalism reign supreme. Hollywood and the media elite move forward with their agenda.

Recently, the release of top-secret Soviet documents in the *Washington Post* shows definitely "a worldwide 'conspiracy' really did exist for much of the past seven decades, with the Kremlin secretly funding client [Communist parties] from India to El Salvador." And we know well the record of how they assisted Gus Hall and the United States Communist Party right up until the last few years.

And what has New World Order-proponent George Bush been doing about the Communist, and now socialist, growth worldwide—while he has been presiding over the largest spending, the most taxes, the biggest budget deficits and growth of big government bureaucracy and regulation in history?

Bush has been helping to fund socialism here and abroad.

We cannot forget the legacy and record of Soviet Communism, because it lives on. It is a legacy of tens of millions killed, thousands of clergy killed, tens of thousands of churches destroyed. It is a legacy of bribery, corruption, black marketeering, lying, cheating, stealing, learning how *not* to work, mistrust of one another, loss of religious faith and traditions of integrity and spirituality. It will take generations for real freedom to come and for the damage to be healed, because the greatest damage done was not to the economies, but to the human psyche and human spirit.

What has kept Communism in power all these years are the unindicted co-conspirators or fellow travelers. And this evil is still being idealized and glorified, in part, even now, because no Nuremberg Trials have taken place for the Communist killers. That is because the current heads of state of the old Communist governments were Communist killers or collaborators themselves, aided by the West. There is a double standard in the West: it is wrong when Nazis kill people, but not wrong when Communists kill people.

And we must never stop asking: where were the leading churchmen in the United States and West during all this death and destruction? Where were the major media elite in the West during all this death and destruction—the greatest in the history of the world? Where were our teachers and professors, and what are they doing today? They are saying the same things, doing the same things.

One observer put it this way: there ought to be a political and intellectual reckoning in the West. We should remember and expose those who argued that the United States was as bad or worse than the Soviet Union; that we are an imperialist nation bent on subjugating the world; that Marxism works better than capitalism in fulfilling human needs; or that Fidel Castro or the Nicaraguan Sandinistas, still wielding power, and Mao Tse Tung represented a bright future for mankind.

Those who promoted the Communist line were disastrously wrong, but in most cases they have not recanted. To the contrary, they and their soul mates are still arguing on college campuses, from pulpits in churches, and in books and magazines, that this country is inherently racist, sexist, corrupt, and oppressive. We have had to put up with this trash for a generation or more, and it is high time that our sons and daughters are no longer subjected to it.

Finally, if we are to change this situation and help preserve America, we must act now. And we must remember that the lesser of evils is still evil.

It's never too late to do the right thing. The best thing we can do is support the Taxpayers Party and a great American patriot, Howard Phillips, in the long-term mission to rescue America from its internal enemies, to save our constitutional republic before it is too late, and to proclaim our belief in our families, our belief in God, our belief in America and freedom.

9. TRUE COMMON LAW

Dr. Ron Paul

When most individuals go to Washington, they need to be there several years before we can accurately assess their effectiveness. Congress has a way of changing a man's convictions. The first year or two is not a good measurement.

The first year I was there, I was definitely determined that I was opposed to big government. In the first year, I did a good job and I voted against spending and I voted against taxes and I won the National Taxpayers Union award, but I had an 82. Eighty-two means that 82 percent of the time I voted against government spending and government taxes, which sounds pretty reasonable, especially since the next best score was a 72, and most congressmen scored closer to 32. By my last year, after eight years, my score was 99. The question is, does that make me an anarchist?

No. I went in the right directions, as far as I'm concerned. Instead of endorsing more government,

I actually came to the conclusion that there was more waste and corruption, that nothing deserved passage.

I have to admit, though, that I'm not an anarchist, and I wouldn't vote for a complete removal of government. But I would be satisfied if we could get rid of about 80 percent.

Another good test of a politician is to see where he goes when he leaves. After my four terms, I went back home; I didn't stay in Washington. Many will stay and live off the system more lucratively than when they were representatives.

A letter came from the Department of Social Services to a gentleman who had recently died, dealing with food stamps. It read: "Your food stamps will be stopped because we received notice that you passed away."

I didn't make this up. And the government bureaucrat goes on to say in the letter, "May God bless you."

It gets worse. "You may reapply if there is a change in your circumstances."

I don't think you have to remember anything else other than that letter to know what's going on in Washington.

We went through an era where we worried about nuclear annihilation, we worried about the hydrogen bomb, and then about a neutron bomb.

Now there's another bomb that has been rumored to be available, and in a way there may be some benefits to this one. This is supposedly an electromagnetic bomb, a Cruise missile generating devastating electromagnetic fields that can knock out power plants and transmission towers as it flies over, while destroying all data stored in tapes and disks. Can you imagine what we could do to the IRS with that one?

Fire can be a real blessing to civilization. It also can destroy us. Nuclear power is the same way. And it is the same way with the computer industries. Computers can be a great help and blessing to all of us in our businesses, but they also can be dangerous weapons in the hands of government agencies.

I'm not going to recite the IRS abuses that you have read about where people lose their property over minor infractions. We've all read those stories. Frequently the taxpayer has made a careless error (and sometimes of course the government could be in error). But now they are becoming much more sophisticated. It isn't only the IRS that is being used to intimidate us. In the last several years they have adopted a procedure where property is seized by the government without due process of law, and it's occurring more rapidly all the time, more *often* all the time. And it's not necessarily done by the IRS.

I know some of you probably have heard of the Financial Crimes Enforcement Agency, which is systematically accumulating material on all Americans on their financial transactions. This has been a tremendous transition from the 1970s when the RICO Act was established. Some of the current things that are going on occurred in 1984 with the Crime Control Act. That was near the end of my time in Congress, and I can remember how it passed. One part of the bill had come up as an individual piece of legislation, and it involved the elimination of the Fourth Amendment, the search-and-seizure protection that we have. It literally rejected the idea that you had to have a search warrant to be searched and there had to be a just cause for being searched.

By alerting other members of Congress when it came up as an individual bill, we were able to prevent it from being passed. But by 1984, during the heat of the campaign in October, when everyone was anxious to leave on a recommittal motion, somebody introduced the Crime Control package, which was 500 pages long and was not available on the House floor in print. Each side had five minutes on this bill of 500 pages—with no debate, and it wasn't even printed. It passed, and it established of a lot of the procedures that are now attacking the property rights of American citizens, and most of the time it's being done in the name of drug control. The war on drugs is the biggest hoax on the American people because it is designed to invade our privacy, control our financial transactions, and it does no good in the war on drugs.

One woman who became aware of the fact that her children were involved in drug usage did what a good mother thought she was supposed to do. She said: "Kids, you've got to leave. I'm not going to have drugs in this house. Get out." She notified the authorities, and she said: "We've had drugs here, and I don't want drugs in my house, and I put my kids out." And she did everything possible to correct the situation.

The DEA came and observed and monitored her house for two weeks, and then seized her house for participating in the drug business. She was never charged with a crime, never convicted of a crime. It was up to her to seek redress and try to get her property back.

This is not uncommon. It is getting more common all the time. Under the IRS, you are guilty until proven innocent.

The *Houston Chronicle* reported a story about an elderly couple who wanted to retire and enjoy themselves. They wanted to move to a smaller house. So they sold their house. They sold it on time. The individual who was paying them got involved in drugs. They lost their house. The property became the crime. The government seized the property, ignoring all sense of property rights and totally ignoring the Constitution.

One of the writers of the 19th century that has influenced me is Lysander Spooner. He had some good ideas about what the role of government ought to be, and he was a strong proponent of common law. He said that there are two main elements of common law. First is trial by jury. There's a good movement in this country today to restore the real notion of trial by jury, which literally means that, ultimately, the test of the law will be by the jury. The jury will not judge guilt or innocence by the information spoon fed to it by a judge, but it should be able to hear any kind of evidence it wants and then it can judge the law itself.

The other element of true common law that Lysander Spooner wrote about is that no taxes should be levied on a free person without his or her consent.

He likened his ideal tax system to that of buying insurance from a mutual insurance company. If you liked what you were getting, you sent them the money; if you didn't, you refrained from sending your premium the next year. Spooner was disappointed about the direction of the country back in the 1850s. I wonder how the poor man would feel today.

Spooner has correct ideas on taxes and trial by jury, but he also taught me something else about the Second Amendment. His explanation of the Second Amendment is rather clear. He said the Second Amendment was not put there so that people could defend themselves against criminals that were coming to rob them. The Second Amendment wasn't established so people could go hunting. *Everybody* went hunting. He states that the Second Amendment was there because their greatest fear and their greatest threat was the government.

He goes on to explain. He says it's obvious that everybody has the right to have food in their houses and the right to have food means you have the right to eat it. Therefore you have the right to own the gun. You also have the right and the obligation, if government's become oppressive, to use the gun.

I do not advocate that, but remember that Otto Scott blamed the Civil War on the intellectual endorsement of the killings by John Brown. Isn't a similar thing happening today? The intellectuals are endorsing the hoodlums in the streets and the riots in Los Angeles, so we have to face up to the fact that we may have riots in the streets. We must do our very best, therefore, to change things peaceably and that's why we have Howard Phillips doing his best to bring about changes in a peaceful manner.

Spooner explains that, if you lose either element of common law—trial by jury or taxation with permission—you always lose both. One leads to the other. And we essentially have neither today. And, if people don't have the right to stand up against their administrative officials—in the House, the Senate, the courts, or in the White House—it will do nothing but lead to tyranny.

This is the direction in which we're headed. Every day we have more tyrannical laws and regulations. We don't own our land. We pay rent to the government for our land. So it gets worse continuously. This is fulfilling the desires and the promotions of those who believe in big government. This has come about in a very deliberate manner.

If there was not a plan by those who were in charge to expand the size and the scope of government, there would not have been the need to introduce two great evils: the personal income tax on our income, as well as the Federal Reserve system.

All we have to do is look at what's happened since then. The monetary cycles are getting worse, and the booms get bigger and the crashes get worse, and we are still in the midst of a very serious crunch. It's been two or three years of the ordinary stimulus of injecting new currency and new cash and new credit, and lowering interest rates. It has not made the economy and the business people respond.

The 20th century has been different from Spooner's time in another way. In the old days, big government was represented by the kings and the dictators, and it was easy for the people to be outraged as they were being taxed because they were being taxed for the king's sake.

But in the 20th century it became more sophisticated. They introduced this modern idea that the purpose was to have government get bigger to take care of the people *for the good of the people*. The liberalism of the 20th century, the New Deal, is always designed to say that those who do not go along with us are evil and immoral and don't care and are unchristian, and we liberals—who are willing to take from one group and give to another—are the only ones who care.

Has it ever dawned on you that those liberals who would take all your guns away are also eager to use the gun of government to take your money and give it to somebody that won't work?

Characteristic of the Federal Reserve system and the deliberate destruction of honest money, inflation is nothing more than a sinister tax because it taxes you without a direct taxation. They print the money and, of course, dilute the value and distort the economy. It works for a while and that's why it is such a great political gimmick. It's a great political system. That is, for a while—as long as they have wealth to consume. There was great wealth in this country because we had a relatively free market. We had a relatively sound currency. But what has happened in the last 50 to 70 years? The money's been undermined and the productivity of the country has been destroyed through this welfare transfer system and the destruction of the monetary system.

So things have changed. People are getting poorer. I happen to side with the liberals who are always challenging some of those so-called conservatives in power that yes, there are more people poor in this country than there were 10 to 15 years ago. I think the standard of living has gone down deliberately and steadily since 1971, since we severed the last linkage to the gold standard. We are worse off, and the people are hurting, and that's why they're angry. This system of taxation is looking more like the old system which was only designed to serve the kings. No, the people aren't benefitting any more and they're angry and they're upset and they want to throw the rascals out.

But the great threat today is that they don't quite understand what they need to replace it. We need a system of liberty; we need a system of strictly limiting the powers of government. But so many people only want to throw the bums out, cut the bums' pay, and make sure they personally get their own check.

When I was in Washington, very seldom did I have individuals coming to lobby me asking for liberty, but I frequently had them coming asking for *things*. The worst group of people to lobby me for largesse were business people. The Chamber of Commerce came. Why aren't you voting for highway funds? Why don't you vote for port funds? Why won't you do this? Why won't you do that?

The larger the business, usually the closer they were aligned with government. Those who were looking for Export-Import Bank loans and subsidies were always involved.

Today we have a real struggle, and it's occurring because the pie is getting smaller. Productivity is down; the currency isn't working; there are international conflicts. There is a struggle now to have a one-world government. But the leeches are very concerned that they're not going to get a check. The producers are waking up.

It eventually came to the point in the Soviet Union where they could not depend on the Soviet government to keep things together and keep the food coming and the thing fell apart. Eventually that will happen here, but will the people then accept a totalitarian government and an iron fist, or are the people going to accept *our* ideas and say that government's role should be changed?

When a social group comes together, whether designed by race or sex or age or ethnic group, they demand certain things because they belong to this group and they want government to take care of them. But if you and I get together and reject this notion on principle, they say we're bigots, which is not fair, not correct. They are the ones who are the real bigots because they are demanding certain privileges at the point of a gun from those who are willing to work.

As the economic pie gets smaller, the government has no recourse but to do what it's doing. The totalitarian role of the government becomes more forceful because it must collect more revenues. There's a limit to how much they can inflate, because the dollar will get too weak. They're trying very desperately to create more productivity, and that's why they have to squeeze out every nickel they can. This is why financial privacy is on the wane and might disappear. There's a chance that if we don't succeed, we will have a cashless society. If not, we have already seen that there have been changes in the currency so that they can monitor and trace every currency, every cash transaction. These trends will continue unless we do something about it.

The movement in the last few years has been beneficial because the American people have expressed their outrage about the taxing authorities, and there's been a taxpayer's bill of rights. I supported a taxpayer's bill of rights. But isn't it tragic that we can't use the *first* Bill of Rights? That's all we need to do.

There's one question that we as a nation and we as a generation must ask and then answer. The key question is: What should the role of government be? What is the role of government?

Those who are in charge of the other two parties and those who are in charge of Washington have an idea what the role of government should be. It's to police the world, police our private and religious lives, and it's to regulate the economy. We should reject this totally. Very simply, the role of government ought to be for the preservation of a natural right to our liberty—nothing more.

The libertarian notion that we reject all aggression is, I think, a proper notion. You can do anything you want with your lives. And with the economy, everything should be voluntary. Don't cheat, don't defraud, and don't hurt somebody, and we'll all get along fairly well. When individuals defraud or cheat or injure or threaten to injure, then the government has a role to play. Accepting Lysander Spooner's two principles of the true common law would go a long way to improving this country.

10. THE MORAL ORDER IN AMERICA

R. J. Rushdoony

I was about eight years old when I came face to face very vividly with the uniqueness of this country. It was in the mid-1920s when my father, a Protestant pastor, went to the Detroit, Michigan, railroad station to meet a friend from the old country. He was originally from Armenia but had recently come to the United States after living in several countries in Europe. There in the station walking with my father, this man, a priest in the church of Armenia, stopped in shock at one street car transfer point, and stood transfixed watching a common American sight. School children who were being escorted across the street by a policeman were vying for the privilege of holding his hand. As he watched the children chatter happily with the policeman, the priest began to weep tears of joy.

Later at the dinner table he said that he now understood the meaning of America, a place where the police represented not a dreaded knock on the door, but protection. Where they were not feared, but liked.

The memory of that episode has been with me over the years. It epitomizes the meaning of this country for me. This does not mean that, when it happened in the early twenties, there were no problems, nor over the years before. I can recall that just a short time earlier, as a very small boy, I had pulled the covers over my head and huddled with fear as a gang of hoodlums broke our windows after dark, venting their hatred on our house because we were foreigners. It was not pleasant, but we all knew there was more to America than that, and we saw that in the response of the neighbors. We knew, because we were an immigrant family coming from persecution and massacre, that America was a moral order. America represented moral order.

Foreign commentators and some of our own scholars have expressed contempt for the American tradition which insists that a moral premise must govern us in all spheres of our political life. As a university student, I would hear contempt for the idea that our State Department should be a force for moral order. We were no longer, the professor said, a country of farmers and small towns, but a cosmopolitan and international culture which should jettison old moralisms. And so we did, to our own disillusionment and international contempt. In the late 1950s and very early 1960s, most of the older generation of Armenian adult immigrants, my father's generation, began to die. I recall being present on one occasion when my father and other older, old-country friends shed tears over the news because they saw what was happening as the moral decline of the United States. One man feared, he said, that we would become another evil force like the Turkish Empire.

That grief is shared now to some degree by many Americans. Freedom is waning. Tyranny is increasing. Not only is statist, centralist power increasing, but it is becoming more and more immoral, more and more evil. I believe, however, that the temper of the 1990s will be an increasing hunger for a return to moral order. Because man is, in the Biblical perspective, a fallen creature, law is seen as basic to society and freedom. The very first German law book in history, the *Saxonspiegel* from around 1220, declared that God is Himself law, and therefore law is dear to Him. They were referring, of course, to God's law. But it's against this that our U.S. Supreme Court has ruled, barring this year any reference in the courts to the Bible's requirement of capital punishment. Because any such reference introduces an outside authority, God, above and beyond the state and its courts.

This sums up the problem tellingly. For humanism the only source of order and law can be man and the state. But man is fallen and immoral. The state reflects man's nature in its corruption. The United States as a moral force is thus a spent force. And its renewal is an urgent necessity.

There are two conflicting perspectives that govern man and the state. The first is the Biblical premise that man is a fallen creature. His personal, societal, and his civil existence manifests a tendency to lawlessness and evil. Given this presupposition, we cannot trust man, the state, the church, or any other agencies. Man's evil bent will function in all these arenas. This means that in all spheres of life man must be subject to God's law as a restraining power. Despite some inconsistencies in his position, Jean Francois Revel, in his recent book *The Flight From Truth: The Reign of Deceit in the Age of Information*, states: "The foremost of all the forces that drive the world today is falsehood." Neither man nor the state are to be trusted. As some of our coinage declares: "In God we trust." We do so because it is dangerous to trust in man or the state. But second, the prevailing belief in our era is derived from Jean Jacques Rousseau, and it is a firm faith in man, in the general will of men, as embodied in the state from which salvation comes. In the eyes of many thinkers since Hegel, the state is God walking on earth. This faith sees man's salvation as requiring that vast powers be surrendered to the state to enable it to accomplish its planning, which is the bureaucratic equivalent for salvation.

These two views lead to varied conclusions. The Biblical faith leads to the kind of statement made in Justinian's code: "It is a statement worthy of the majesty of a reigning Prince for him to profess to be subject to the Laws. For our authority is dependent upon that of the Law." As against this is the pagan Roman view that whatever has pleased the prince has the force of law and is absolved from the laws. The Supreme Court has made this a premise of the federal government. In the modern perspective, this has meant that any state which claims to be a sovereign power above the law cannot be bound by law. The U.S. Constitution avoided all claims to sovereignty because it belongs to God alone. But the courts have re-introduced this doctrine which Washington at the Constitutional Convention ruled out of order.

As a result, now no law or amendment against deficit spending can prevail, because the sovereign power cannot be bound by law. The state then becomes a law, and what it wills is therefore right, at least for the moment. Given the premise of Rousseau we find ourselves in the same camp as Stalin and Hitler. The difference is now one of degree, not of kind. We are on the road to serfdom and tyranny, from which there is no escape unless we look to a transcendental source, moral order.

America is disappearing rapidly as a moral order, and the power state as man's order is replacing it. Law and government are rooted in the faith of the people. It is time for us to seek a change in ourselves, in our laws, and in our civil government. In every sphere American society faces rapid disintegration. Our trust has too long been in tried and tested failures. The causes, parties, and men whom we have trusted have cynically pursued courses alien to our heritage. They will soon leave us with no heritage except a power state which seeks to crush us and our freedom. The state is not the source of moral order, and we must change directions before it is too late.

In the mid-1980s, at a national meeting of prominent conservatives, I saw clearly the bankruptcy of present-day conservative leaders. I overheard some men in politics comment on Howard Phillips. They agreed that he is outstanding in every respect, but they also agreed that he was not in tune with politics because he fought losing issues such as South Africa, abortion, and other matters on moral grounds. For these men, the sound approach was to take the right stance on such issues but without any commitment of time, effort, or money. Please the people and do nothing. Say what they want and then disregard them.

This episode tells us why we are losing. As John Lofton has observed, the conservative position today is too often the leftist one of ten years ago. It is essentially unprincipled and opportunistic.

This has never been the approach of Howard Phillips. He is a man to respect and to support and that is why I cast my lot with him.

11. THROW THE HYPOCRITICAL RASCALS OUT

Jack Gargan

Howard Phillips was one of the very first to have faith in me, and he has always been there to help me when I needed it, and I'm very grateful to him for that.

As you may know, "THRO" is the acronym for "Throw the Hypocritical Rascals Out." It's an anti-incumbency movement directed primarily at Congress.

I'm just one guy, and I'm spread pretty thin, so I can't take everybody on. But I've been concerned for 30 years at the direction in which this country has been going. Finally I decided to do something. Two and a half years ago, just before the 1990 election campaign, I got more than just concerned. I got activated.

When Congress pulled a pay raise scam on us in the middle of the night, and then when the S&L scam hit us and everything was coming apart, I thought, "Hey, somebody's got to do something, or we're going to lose this country for all those good kids."

That's why I started THRO. I took some money out of my retirement, just about all of it, and bought seven newspaper ads. The thrust of the ads said simply that we send good people to Congress, and the seniority system there seems to do one of two things to them:

1. It totally frustrates them if they refuse to compromise their principles, so that they bail out in relatively short fashion.

2. Being human beings, they adjust to an old saying in Congress: "If you want to get along, you'd better go along."

That is why we're on the brink of the most incredible financial catastrophe the world has ever seen. Immorality is running rampant on Capitol Hill. Although I'm the first to say there are abuses of government from the president down to the dog catcher—*nobody* is immune out there—Congress is at the root of the problem.

This can be illustrated by today's installment of the good news/bad news syndrome. The good news is that at last, Saddam Hussein is going to be tried for war crimes. The bad news is that he's going to be tried by the Senate Ethics Committee!

I watched as much as I could of the Democratic and the Republican conventions. As I sat there, I could not remember when I had seen so many otherwise bright-looking people being taken in so completely and so quickly.

Then I remembered. It was at the *last* Democratic and Republican conventions! And the ones before that and the ones before that.

I've been on the political scene now since I cast my first vote for Dwight D. Eisenhower when I was in the service during the Korean War in 1952, and I have faithfully watched the political process ever since—much to my dismay, most of the time.

Just about that time, a cartoon made its first appearance in the papers; it was called "Peanuts." From the beginning, Lucy would tee up the ball at the start of football season, and she'd say, "Come on Charlie Brown, kick this ball!"

At first he'd coming running and at the last second, she'd snatch the ball out of the way and he'd end up on his tail. Every year you figured, "Come on, Charlie Brown, you're going to wise up one of these days."

But every year, Lucy conned Charlie Brown. She'd say, "Charlie, I promise you, *this time* I won't pull the ball away."

Now here it is, football season, and Lucy is going to tee up the ball and say to Charlie Brown, "Come on, Charlie, kick this ball."

So help me, he's going to do it again.

Sadly, that's the story of American politics. Every four years the Republicans and the Democrats get up there and say, "Come on, America, look at our platform, look at all of these great things. We're going to turn the country around in 100 days—health care for all, prosperity for all, liberty for all. We're going to repair the infrastructure;

we're going to get rid of all the crime and drugs; we're going to do this, we're going to do that."

This time, the Democrats' theme was: "Don't look back, don't look back! We're looking to the future!"

Do you know why they don't want you to look back? Because it's the same crowd that got you into this fix that is now telling you they're going to lead you out of it!

And then there are the Republicans. "Read my lips—no new taxes." I call that, in the phraseology today, "the mother of all political lies." So much for family values. In my family, we were taught that you don't tell lies. And yet, you and I got stuck for $165 billion in new taxes. Middle America took it on the chin.

We just witnessed the devastation of Hurricane Andrew. It was the worst natural disaster, in terms of dollar value, that this nation has ever seen. Some people estimate that it brought between $20-30 billion of damage. Even today, Miami looks like a war zone. As far as you can see, in some places, there is not a vehicle, there is not a home, there is not a building standing. Total destruction. But for the grace of God, the death toll would have been staggering.

Amazingly though, the Republican's "no new taxes" administration has dumped on us 6.6 Hurricane Andrews.

This was the very year that the Comptroller General of the United States, backed up by the Grace Commission and Citizens Against Waste in Government estimated there was $180 billion of sheer government waste in fiscal year 1991 alone. That's another 7.2 Andrews.

It is no wonder then that folks are waking up, and they're starting to say, "We can take our country back from these career politicians."

When I was foolish enough to take those first seven newspaper ads out, I said: "One person cannot make a difference, but you and I together can." And that is the truth. Together we can indeed make a difference for our kids and grandkids. And it's about time.

I'm the guy whose ads say: "I'm mad as hell and I'm not going to take it any more." I meant it, and I still do.

Within 132 days from the time the first ad ran at the end of June 1990 until election day, November 6, 1990, the good people of middle America sent me enough money to buy another 245 full-page ads covering this country. And some of those ads were very expensive, such as those in *USA Today*, which cost $55,000 a page.

Amazingly, those donations came almost entirely in $5, $10, and $25 increments. The biggest single contribution was $5,000. The next biggest was $1,200. All the rest came from middle America—$5, $10, and $25.

I'm happy to tell you that this kind of support has continued. The THRO campaign has now been running for two-and-a-half years, and I have spent less money than one Congressman in one congressional district.

Just last week I started my new "mad as hell" ad campaign. My goal is to place 400 campaign ads across the country. We hope to be able to replace quite a few hypocritical rascals in Congress and thus to begin the process of renewal in America.

We can't have a war between the president and the Congress any more; we have got to get sanity back into our government. My job, as I see it, is to turn over as many folks up there at the congressional level as we possibly can. They have put our country at risk. And it cannot continue.

Two years ago, when I started this speaking tour, I used to say, "Do you know your Congressman is out there spending $9,000 a second more than we're taking in?" A year ago I had to change it, and say, "Do you know your Congressman is spending $12,000 a second more than we're taking in?" Today, I have to make another revision. Now your Congressman is spending $15,900 a second more than this great nation can bring in.

You can't run a country like that. We are now $4 trillion in debt. It was the late Senator Everett Dirkson who once said: "A billion here, a billion there, and pretty soon we're going to be talking real money." He didn't even think in terms of trillions, and that wasn't that long ago. Not only are we *thinking* in terms of trillions—*we are there*.

If you started in business the day that Christ was born and you were such a rotten business person that you lost a million dollars a day, do you know when you would have lost your first trillion dollars? You wouldn't have lost it yet. It'll be the year 2740 before you lose your first trillion dollars. This incredible, insane Congress of ours has put this nation down the toilet for $3 trillion in 10 years. And there was a trillion already in the hopper. Four trillion dollars! That's $16,000 per person for everybody in this country. Every new baby born in America starts out owing $16,000.

Somebody, somehow has got to put a stop to this madness. If not us, then who? If not now, then when?

Let's throw the hypocritical rascals out. And let's do it now.

U.S. TAXPAYERS PARTY: 1992 PLATFORM

We, the members of the U.S. Taxpayers Party, gratefully acknowledge the blessings of the Lord God as Creator, Preserver, and Ruler of the Universe and of this Nation. We hereby appeal to Him for aid, comfort, guidance and the protection of His Divine Providence as we work to restore and preserve this nation as a government of the people, for the people, and by the people.

The U.S. Constitution established a republic under God, rather than a democracy.

Our republic is a nation governed by a Constitution which is rooted in Biblical law, administered by representatives of the Constitution democratically elected by the citizens.

In a republic governed by constitutional law rooted in Biblical law, all life, liberty, and property are safe because law rules.

We affirm the principles of inherent individual rights upon which these United States of America were founded:

- That each individual is endowed by his Creator with certain inalienable rights, that among these are the right to life, liberty, property and the pursuit of the individual's personal interest so long as such pursuits do not trespass on the equal rights of others;

- That the freedom to own, use, exchange, control, protect and freely dispose of property is a natural, necessary, and inseparable extension of the individual's inalienable rights;

- That the legitimate function of government is to safeguard those rights through the preservation of domestic tranquility, the maintenance of a strong national defense and the promotion of equal justice for all;

- That history makes clear that, left unchecked, it is the nature of government to usurp the liberty of its citizens and eventually become a major violator of the people's rights; and

- That, therefore, it is essential to bind government with the chains of the Constitution and carefully divide and jealously limit government's powers to those assigned by the consent of the governed.

The U.S. Taxpayers Party calls on all who love liberty and value their inherent rights to join with us in the pursuit of these goals and the restoration of these founding principles. We speak for the majority of Americans: hardworking, productive, taxpaying men and women who constitute the backbone, and the heart, of the American republic and its economy.

These are the producers; these are the ones who should be "first considered and always remembered." It is on their backs that government is carried and it is out of their pockets that government is financed. Without them and without the product of their skills and their labors, there would be no source to fund the legitimate functions of government and no charity to support the private institutions helping those in need.

No nation can survive if it fails to honorably address the problems which concern these citizens. To these productive but generally forgotten Americans, we offer this platform. It responds to their desires; it is the voice which speaks of them and for them as does that of no other political party.

ABORTION

The first duty of the law is to prevent the shedding of innocent blood. America's Founding Fathers emphasized that the Constitution of the United States was ordained and established for "ourselves and our posterity." Article IV of the Constitution guarantees to each state a republican form of government. In a republic, the taking of innocent life may not be authorized by any institution of government—legislative, judicial, or executive. Our right to life may certainly not properly be made dependent upon the vote of a majority of any legislative body. The unborn child is a human person created in God's image. The duty of civil government is to safeguard from assault each such precious life. We oppose any assignment of federal funds to organizations, domestic or foreign, which advocate, encourage, or participate in the practice of abortion. We will only appoint to the federal judiciary and positions of authority in the Department of Justice qualified individuals who publicly acknowledge the personhood of the unborn child. We support enactment of laws to reverse those statutes and judicial decisions which now provide for abortion on demand.

AIDS

The spread of AIDS is attributable to various causes, but principally to promiscuous homosexual conduct and drug abuse. Because of the failure of the federal government to protect the blood supply under its control from corruption, and because of policies which in fact encourage illicit sexual conduct and which otherwise place innocent citizens at risk, millions of non-homosexual, non-drug-abusing Americans have been given a death sentence.

Under no circumstances should the federal government continue to subsidize activities which have the effect of encouraging homosexual conduct. In the name of "safe sex," hundreds of millions of tax dollars have been misdirected to organizations which contribute to the spread of AIDS by endorsing, implicitly and explicitly, perverse, unhealthy sexual conduct.

In all federally-funded facilities and institutions, the policy of the United States government should be to protect the uninfected from any avoidable exposure which could place them at risk, not only for the HIV virus and AIDS, but to all of the diseases which are direct and indirect by-products of promiscuous sexual behavior and drug abuse. We believe that HIV infection is a public health concern, and not a civil rights issue.

Criminal penalties should apply to those whose willful acts of omission or commission place members of the public at toxic risk.

BRING GOVERNMENT BACK HOME

The closer civil government is to the people, the more responsible, responsive, and accountable it is likely to be. The Tenth Amendment to the Constitution makes clear that the federal government has only those functions which are explicitly assigned to it. All other rights and authorities are reserved to the states and to the people. We pledge to be faithful to this constitutional requirement and to work methodically to restore to the states and to the people control over legislative, judicial, executive, and regulatory functions which are beyond the proper scope of the federal government.

CONGRESSIONAL REFORM

The Congress of the United States has become an overpaid, overstaffed, self-serving institution. It confiscates taxpayer funds to finance exorbitant salaries, pensions and perks. Most members of Congress have become more accountable to the Washington Establishment than to the people in their home districts. Both Houses of Congress are all too often unresponsive and irresponsible, arrogantly placing themselves above the very laws they enact and beyond the control of the citizens they have sworn to represent and serve.

It is time for the American people to renew effective supervision of their employees in public office, to restore right standards, and to take back their government. Congress must once again be accountable to the people.

The U.S. Taxpayers Party calls for implementation of the following agenda to facilitate such reform:

- Apply to Congress all laws it has enforced upon the private citizens (civil rights, labor laws, environmental laws, etc.);
- Abolish Congressional pensions;
- Abolish federal pay for members of Congress and restore provisions for *per diem* allowances;
- Abolish or severely restrict the franking privilege;
- Abolish the 1974 Federal Election Law and the General Election Commission;
- Make it easier and less expensive for new political parties and candidates to get on the ballot.

We support the opportunity of free citizens to apply term limits to all elected officials and Executive Branch, administrative personnel.

CONSTITUTIONAL CONVENTION

We oppose any attempt to call for a constitutional convention for any purpose whatsoever because it cannot be limited to any single issue and such convention could seriously erode our constitutionally protected inalienable rights.

COST OF BIG GOVERNMENT

The only legitimate purpose of civil government is to safeguard the God-given rights of its citizens: namely, life, liberty and property. Only those duties, functions, and programs specifically assigned to the federal government by the Constitution should be funded.

In the past 30 years, federal spending has increased from less than $100 billion a year in 1961 to $1.5 *trillion* for the current fiscal year.

Consider this:

- Since 1988, the number of pages required in the federal *Register* to list all new regulations has zoomed from 53,376 pages to 67,716 in 1992.

- The number of federal employees involved in issuing and enforcing regulations has increased from 104,360 in 1988 to an all-time high of 124,994 in 1992.

- The amount of taxpayer money the federal leviathan spends each year administering the jungle of regulations has increased from $9.6 billion in 1988 to $11.3 billion in 1992.

- Federal regulations are now costing the American people between $881 billion and $1.65 trillion a year.

The federal government has turned into a tax-and-spend monster which is devouring the people it is supposed to be serving.

As the Declaration of Independence cried out, so it is today: The federal government "has erected a multitude of new offices, and sent hither swarms of officers to harass our people and eat out their substance." Just since 1961, 297 new federal commissions, councils, public corporations, grants, and management programs have been created—in addition to all those which existed beforehand. In addition, more than 60 new boards and commissions were empowered.

The U.S. Taxpayers Party calls on all citizens to join in the drive to restore constitutional government and reduce the cost and controls of the federal leviathan. We must reduce the reach, the grasp, and the take of the federal government. It has grown too big, too expensive, too wasteful, too arrogant. It is a government which has become unaccountable and unresponsive to the people.

We must restore to the states those powers, programs, and sources of revenues which the federal government has usurped.

The U.S. Taxpayers Party calls upon the Congress and the Executive to disapprove and halt all federal expenditures which are not specifically authorized by the Constitution of these United States.

We call for abolition of a Civil Service system which confers a "property right" on jobs as government employees. The President should be able to determine who will carry out—free from subversion or opposition by tax-paid personnel—those programs which he has promised the people to inaugurate and implement.

Turning back the "federal spending clock" by five years will not destroy the economy; in fact, it would revive it. Instead of having these monies confiscated and squandered by politicians and bureaucrats, we would return hundreds of billions of dollars to the taxpayers, so that Americans could spend or invest their own money as they chose. The productive private sector jobs created and the investment capital released would not only put new life in the domestic economy, it would be an important assist in the drive to compete with foreign industries here and in world markets. The return of the people's money would create jobs and investments instead of having it confiscated and spent on non-productive, wasteful programs and pork barrels by politicians and bureaucrats.

CRIME

Crime in most cases is to be dealt with by state and local governments. To the degree that the federal government, in its legislation, in its judicial actions, in its regulations, and in its Executive Branch activities, interferes with the ability of the people in their communities to apprehend, judge, and penalize accused lawbreakers, it bears responsibility for the climate of crime which has grown more destructive with each passing year.

We favor the unimpeded right of states and localities to execute criminals convicted of capital crimes and to require restitution for the victims of criminals who have not threatened the lives or physical safety of others. Federal interference with local criminal justice processes should be limited to that which is constitutionally required.

DEFENSE

It is a primary obligation of the federal government to provide for the common defense, vigilant to deal with significant potential threats and prospective capabilities, as well as with perceived present intentions.

We oppose the unilateral dismantlement and dismemberment of America's defense infrastructure. That which is hastily torn down will not be easily rebuilt.

In order to protect our territory, our armed forces, and our citizenry, we should immediately give the required six-months notice of our withdrawal from the Nixon-Brezhnev Anti-Ballistic Missile Treaty, which restricts full development and deployment of a strategic defense system—the installation of which will be of the highest priority for our party's candidates once elected to office.

Under no circumstances would we commit U.S. forces to serve under any flag but that of the United States of America. We are opposed to any New World Order of the kind conceived by George Bush, and we flatly reject U.S. participation in any New World Army.

The goal of U.S. security policy is to defend the national security interests of the United States.

We should be the friend of liberty everywhere, but the guarantor and provisioner of ours alone.

We urge the Executive and Legislative Branches to continue to provide for the modernization of our Armed Forces in keeping with advancing technologies and a constantly changing world situation.

We call for the maintenance of a strong, state-of-the-art military on land, sea, and in the air, as well for the development and maintenance of a strong space defense system (which could be to the future defense of this nation what the air and naval power are now).

We support the maintenance of a strong and ready and well-equipped Reserve and National Guard.

We call for talks with the Republic of Panama intended to restore to the United States control over the operations and security of the Panama Canal, while fully recognizing the autonomy and independence of the Republic of Panama. Under no circumstances should we unilaterally surrender our military base rights in Panama at a time when the people of Panama desire that we continue them.

DRUG ABUSE

The U.S. Taxpayers Party will uphold the right of states and localities to restrict access to drugs and to enforce such restrictions in appropriate cases with application of the death penalty. We support legislation to stop the flow of illegal drugs into the United States from foreign sources. As a matter of self-defense, retaliatory policies, including embargoes, sanctions, and tariffs, should be considered.

At the same time, we will take care to prevent violations of the constitutional and civil rights of American citizens. Arbitrary searches and seizures must be prohibited and the presumption of innocence must be preserved.

THE ECONOMY

The big issues of 1992 are jobs and the economy. The reason for economic hard times is that government has grown too big, too burdensome, and too expensive.

During the past 30 years:

- income tax collections have increased from $41 billion in 1961 to $468 billion in 1991.
- Social Security taxes have gone up from $16 billion in 1961 to $370 billion in 1991.
- Corporate taxes have gone up from $21 billion in 1961 to $98 billion in 1981.

Since 1981 the national debt has quadrupled: from $914 billion to at least $4 trillion.

In two or three years, it will cost more to service the debt than Uncle Sam collects in income taxes.

The situation is not hopeless. A President who knows what needs to be done, who understands how to do it, and who has the courage to act, can turn the crisis around in the space of a single four-year term.

The result will be more jobs, greater prosperity, less inflation, and lower taxes.

The answer is simple. Let's roll the clock back on federal spending to what it was five years ago, where, instead of spending about $1.5 trillion a year, Uncle Sam was spending one-third less.

That kind of cutback in spending can be achieved by a President willing to use his veto and govern confrontationally against all the special interests which feed at the federal trough.

EDUCATION

All education is inherently religious, in the sense that all teaching is related to basic assumptions about the nature of God and man. God has invested parents with the responsibility for the nurture and training of the children He has entrusted to them. Education should be parentally accountable.

Education should be free from any federal government subsidy and all government interference. The federal government has no legitimate role in either subsidizing or regulating education, except insofar as it relates to members of the Armed Forces and employees of the Executive Branch. Under no circumstances should the federal government involve itself in matters of education curriculum or textbooks.

ELECTION REFORM

The U.S. Taxpayers Party seeks the restoration of an electoral process which is controlled at the state and local level and is beyond manipulation by federal judges and bureaucrats. The federal government has unconstitutionally and unwisely preempted control in matters of district boundaries, electoral procedures, and campaign activities.

Elections should be accountable to the people, not to the government. The Voting Rights Act should be repealed. The Federal Election Commission should be abolished.

Each citizen should have the right to seek public office in accordance with the qualifications set forth in the federal and state Constitutions. Additional restrictions and obligations governing candidate eligibility and campaign procedures unduly burden the fairness and accountability of our political system.

We urge an end to electronic or mechanical voting processes and a return to the manual counting process overseen by and accountable to voters resident in each precinct where the votes are cast.

ENERGY

We call attention to the continuing need of the United States for a sufficient supply of energy to sustain the nation's standard of living and its agricultural, business, and industrial activities.

Private property rights should be respected and government should not interfere with the development of potential energy sources, including hydroelectric power, solar energy, wind generators, and nuclear energy.

We also encourage the use of coal, shale, and oil sands for the production of power and the conversion of coal, shale, and agricultural products to synthetic fuels.

We oppose any increase in federal fuel taxes and insist that, so long as such taxes are collected in any amount, all of their proceeds should be used exclusively for the maintenance of interstate highways.

ENVIRONMENT

It is a prime responsibility of man to be a prudent, productive and efficient steward of God's natural resources. In that role, man is commanded to be fruitful, to multiply, to replenish the earth, and develop it—to turn deserts into farms and wastelands into groves. This requires a proper and continuing dynamic balance between development and conservation, between use and preservation.

The proper exercise of stewardship demands that we avoid the extremes; that we escape the deadly hand of government confiscation; that we recognize and preserve the right of the individual to acquire, own, and use his property so long as he does not infringe on the rights of other individuals to do the same.

The progress and well-being of society requires that the best interests of human beings must be accorded preference to so-called animal rights. This is not to say that the preservation and care of the creatures of the forest, field, and water are not part of stewardship—they are; but when we choose between an owl or a snail darter and the jobs of American citizens and the well-being of their families and children, the families must be valued above plants and animals.

We wholeheartedly support realistic efforts to preserve the environment and reduce pollution—air, water, and land. We reject, however, the argument that this objective ought to be pursued by costly governmental interference, accompanied by multitudes of regulations and the heavy hand of arrogant bureaucrats spurred on by irresponsible pressure groups.

The Constitution of the United States requires that private property owners be compensated for any government "taking" of their property—whether it be through outright confiscation or by the imposition of rules and regulations which preclude the productive use of the property. This mandate must be strictly observed.

We call for the return to the states and to the people all lands which are held by the federal government without authorization by the Constitution.

EUTHANASIA

The U.S. Taxpayers Party is on record as recognizing and putting first the sanctity of human life.

Just as we oppose abortion—the taking of an innocent, pre-born life—so we adamantly oppose assisted murder.

We oppose any laws which condone or would legalize euthanasia, the so-called "mercy killing" of the aged, the ailing, the infirm. The concept of euthanasia is a dangerous move toward legalized termination of the non-productive, the unwanted, and the unprotected. A nation which has become inured to the slaughter of some 30 million innocent babies can all too easily slide into the Hitlerian-Sangerite goal of eliminating those it considers misfits, undesirables or non-productives.

Any physician or nurse who assists in the extinguishment of life is not worthy to be a member of the healing arts profession, which is one of the noblest of all callings.

FOREIGN AID

Ever since World War II, the United States has provided military and non-military aid to more than 100 nations. Hundreds of billions of dollars have been poured down that bottomless pit—with little evident benefit to the safety and security of the American people. Not only have we given aid to our "friends," but to "neutrals" by means of which aid we hoped to buy their "friendship." Finally, we are now committing ourselves to send the taxpayers' dollars to those who have been our enemies for years. This must stop!

The Congress and the President have a duty to provide for the defense of this country, but the American people have no similar duty to provide tax dollars for the defense of any foreign nation. Further, the U.S. government has no right, let alone a duty, to tax the American people to provide aid of any kind to foreign governments.

Therefore the U.S. Taxpayers Party will:

- Terminate *all* programs of foreign aid, whether military or non-military, to *any* other government.
- Dismantle the Agency for International Development within the Department of State.
- Prevent any dollar of the U.S. taxpayers' money from being spent on aid to the former Soviet Union.

FOREIGN POLICY

The only constitutional purpose and basis of foreign policy is to serve the best interests of the nation. It is not to be the world's policeman or play the world's Santa Claus.

We pledge our allegiance to the American Republic. We say "No!" to any so-called New World Order or one-world government. Not one whit of American autonomy may be given up to any international organization or group of nations.

We oppose entangling foreign alliances. The United States should withdraw from NATO and bring our armed forces home from Europe, as well as from Japan and Korea.

We should review all existing treaties to determine which, if any, are beyond constitutional limits; those which are should be rescinded.

The United States must not enter into agreements which would have an adverse impact on the security and safety of this nation. We should immediately renounce all economic sanctions and embargoes against the Republic of South Africa.

The U.S. Taxpayers Party calls on the United States to withdraw from the United Nations and to encourage the UN to move out of the United States.

We believe that the United States should withdraw from all international monetary and financial institutions and agencies such as the International Monetary Fund (IMF), the World Bank, etc.

GUN CONTROL

The right to bear arms is inherent in the right of self defense conferred on the individual by his Creator to safeguard his own life, liberty, and property and that of his family, as well as to help preserve the independence of the nation.

The right to bear arms is guaranteed by the Second Amendment to the Constitution; it may not properly be infringed upon or denied.

The U.S. Taxpayers Party upholds the right of the citizen to keep and bear arms. We oppose attempts to prohibit the ownership of guns by law-abiding citizens, and stand against all laws which would require the registration of guns or ammunition.

We emphasize that when guns are outlawed only the outlaws will have them. In such circumstances, the peaceful citizen's protection against the criminal would be seriously jeopardized.

IMMIGRATION

Each year some 400,000 legal immigrants and another 300,000 illegals enter the United States. These immigrants—including illegal aliens—have been made eligible for various kinds of public assistance, including housing, education, and Social Security, and legal services, while paying few if any taxes. This unconstitutional raid on the federal Treasury is having a severe and adverse impact on our economy, increasing the cost of government at federal and local levels, adding to the tax burden and stressing the fabric of society.

The U.S. Taxpayers Party demands that the federal government restore immigration policies based on the practice that potential immigrants will be disqualified from admission to the U.S. if, on grounds of health, criminality, morals, or financial dependency, they would impose an improper burden on persons already resident in the United States.

We oppose bilingual ballots. We insist that those who wish to take part in the electoral process and governance of this nation should be required to read and comprehend basic English.

We insist that each immigrant who is admitted must have a sponsor who is legally, morally, and financially obliged to bear full responsibility for the economic independence of the immigrant, lest the burden be unfairly shifted to other taxpayers.

We also insist that those groups and private agencies which request the admission of immigrants to the U.S. as political refugees or economic hardship cases be required to legally commit themselves to providing housing and sustenance for such immigrants and to post appropriate bonds to seal such covenants.

We support the strengthening of the Immigration and Naturalization Service for the proper screening of immigrants, the apprehending and deportation of illegal aliens, and the protection of our borders.

We oppose the provision of welfare and other taxpayer-supported benefits to illegal aliens and reject the practice of bestowing U.S. citizenship on children born to illegal alien parents while in this country.

INDIVIDUAL RIGHTS

We oppose laws which enforce discrimination (reverse or otherwise) on the basis of race, color, ethnic origin, age or gender.

We oppose quotas imposed by or applied in any government or public institution.

Each and every citizen should be free to choose his friends and associates, to offer, seek or refuse employment, and to rent or sell his property to whomever he wishes.

MONEY AND BANKING

Money is both a medium of exchange and a measure of a nation's morality.

Properly established and guarded, it provides the citizen with an assured standard by which he can trade (exchange) his labors or property for a service or product he desires to acquire. The improper control (manipulation) of the money and banking system destroys the value of the citizen's earnings and investments and brings untold misery upon the people. Indeed, it can spawn rebellion and anarchy which shatters societies and topples governments.

The Founding Fathers established a system of sound and honest money designed to prohibit "improper and wicked" manipulation of the medium of exchange. Its purpose was to guarantee that the purchasing power of the citizen's earnings would not be diminished or degraded between the time income is earned and the time it is spent; that it will not lose its purchasing power between the time it is invested and the time it is withdrawn.

Over the years, the federal government has radically departed from the constitutional principles of money and banking. The present regime of fiat money provides no restraint on the politicians' and the monetary authorities' power to debase the currency. Indeed, today's monetary system is precisely what the Founding Fathers feared most and sought to prohibit constitutionally.

The results of these violations of the Constitution threaten the economic stability and indeed the survival of America's republican form of government. Fundamental reform of the monetary and banking systems of the United States is imperative if this nation is to regain its political integrity and restore its economic health.

The U.S. Taxpayers Party calls for and sees as vital a return to the money and banking provisions set forth in the Constitution. Those rules define a system of money and banking relying on free market principles and prescribe what must be done:

- Restore, as the nation's official medium of exchange, the *type of money* the world has historically favored—commodity money; money capable of being coined or tendered as coin.

- Re-establish the *quality of money* which the international market recognizes as pre-eminent—silver and gold exclusively as the standard of the money of the United States.

- Adopt again, as the *unit of money*, the sound dollar of 371¼ grains (troy) of fine silver, and

- Leave determination of *the ultimate supply of money* up to the free market system of free coinage embodied in Anglo-American common law.

Further, we believe that, to restore integrity, credibility, and stability of the nation's money and banking system, we must:

1. Declare unconstitutional
   - the Federal Reserve Act of 1913,
   - the seizure of gold coins in 1933, and
   - the outlawing in 1934 of private contracts that called for payment in silver and gold.

2. Disestablish the Federal Reserve System.

3. Terminate the status of Federal Reserve Notes as obligations of the United States and as legal tender for all debts.

4. Restore to the constitutional monetary system that gold which was unconstitutionally seized from the American people in 1933 and which is now held by the U.S. Treasury.

5. Revalue in constitutional (silver) dollars all outstanding contracts now payable in Federal Reserve Notes.

6. Resume the "free coinage" of constitutional (silver) dollars and appropriate gold coins.

7. Adopt all monetarily viable foreign silver and gold coins as money in the United States.

8. Prohibit all fraudulent "fractional reserve" banking schemes and related commercial practices.

NEW WORLD ORDER

We say "No" to the so-called New World Order and "Yes!" to the autonomy of these United States of America.

The U.S. Taxpayers Party strongly opposes any alliance or participation in any treaty or agreement which compromises our independence as a nation or which subverts our Constitution by improperly committing us to participation in foreign conflicts or intervention in foreign wars.

We join with other American patriots to steadfastly oppose the surrender of American liberty and autonomy to any form of world government or any organization which works toward that end.

We call upon the President and the Congress to terminate the membership of the United States in the United Nations and its subsidiary and affiliated organizations.

We further call upon the Congress and—if it refuses to act—upon the several states, to move to amend the Constitution to prohibit the United States government from entering into any treaty or other agreement or covenant which in any way commits American armed forces, or tax money, or decision-making authority to agencies beyond direct accountability to the states and the people.

All treaties must be subordinate to the Constitution since the Constitution is the only act which empowers and limits the federal government.

The Framers assumed, as a matter of course, that treaties would be subordinate. In fact, the stated reason for the particular wording of the Constitution concerning treaties was to make sure preexisting treaties, including the post-Revolutionary peace treaties concluded under the Articles of Confederation, would remain valid.

As pointed out by the late Supreme Court Justice Hugo Black, "The United States is entirely a creature of the Constitution. It can only act in accordance with the limitations imposed by the Constitution. . . . There is nothing in this language (Article VI) which intimates that treaties and laws enacted pursuant to them do not have to comply with the provisions of the Constitution, nor is there anything in the debates which accompanied the drafting and ratification of the Constitution which even suggests such a result."

And Thomas Jefferson, addressing the question directly, had this to say: ". . . Surely the President and Senate can not do by treaty what the whole government is interdicted from doing in any way."

PRIVATIZATION

There is no constitutional basis for the federal government engaging in such enterprises as Amtrak, Conrail, the TVA, or the Oak Ridge uranium enrichment facility.

Further, in violation of Article I, Section 8, Paragraph 17 of the Constitution, the federal government has vast areas of land under federal ownership and control which have nothing to do with the nation's defense or seat of government.

The U.S. Taxpayers Party calls for the federal government to divest itself of operations which are not authorized by the Constitution. We call upon the Congress to get the federal government out of such enterprises which compete with private free enterprise.

In pursuit of these ends, we endorse the ratification of the Liberty Amendment.

We also call for the federal government to divest itself of the millions of acres of lands and natural resources in Alaska and other western states by selling such properties and using the income from such sales only and entirely to reduce the federal debt.

RELIGIOUS FREEDOM

The preservation of religious freedom, and its protection from the acts of Congress and the infringement of the courts may well become the central civil rights issue of the 1990s.

The federal government (and its agencies and courts) continues to restrict the free exercise and expression of religion. The government openly violates the religious guarantees of the First Amendment:

- It seeks to regulate churches and other religious organizations.
- It has, with the backing of the courts, restricted religious liberty in the area of public and private education.
- It has forbidden non-denominational prayer in the public schools and at educational ceremonies.
- It has prohibited students from reading the Bible on school busses or in classrooms.
- It has refused to permit religious displays on public property such as at Christmas and Chanukah.

And in these violations it has generally been upheld by a majority of the politically appointed Supreme Court.

Further, the Congress, with the approval of the Executive Branch, has subjected churches and their employees to Social Security taxes even though Congress is constitutionally forbidden to make any such law respecting an establishment of religion.

In the strongest tones possible, the U.S. Taxpayers Party calls on the courts, the IRS and all other federal and state and local governments to uphold religious freedom in this nation. These attacks against freedom of worship must cease and the harassment of religious institutions must halt.

The federal government must stop its attempts to interfere with the encouragement of religious and moral principles by state and local governments.

We assert that any form of taxation on churches and other religious organizations is a direct and dangerous step toward state control of the church; such intrusion is prohibited by the Constitution and must be halted.

We insist that the original intention of the Framers of the Constitution in regard to the free exercise of religious faith and practice be reasserted.

SOCIALIZED MEDICINE

The U.S. Taxpayers Party opposes the governmentalization and bureaucratization of American medicine. Government regulation and subsidy constitutes a threat to both the quality and the availability of patient-oriented health care and treatment.

Hospitals, doctors, and other health care providers should be accountable to patients—not to politicians.

If the *supply* of medical care is controlled by the federal government, then officers of that government will determine which *demand* is satisfied.

The result will be rationing of services, higher costs, poorer results—and the power of life and death transferred from caring physicians to unaccountable political overseers.

We applaud proposals for employee-controlled "family coverage" health insurance plans based on cash value life insurance principles.

We affirm freedom of choice of practitioner, and treatment for all citizens with any health problem.

SOCIAL SECURITY

The Social Security trust should not be a rainy-day fund which politicians can pirate or from which they can borrow to cover their errors and pay for their excesses.

The U.S. Taxpayers Party supports legislation to require that the federal government meet its obligations and protect Social Security funds as a trust which can be used only to fulfill its obligations to those who have contributed to the system.

To protect and enhance the return on payments made by Social Security taxpayers and prevent future defaults, we call for the transfer of all Social Security funds to accounts beyond the reach of politicians who improperly transfer funds from Social Security to help pay the price of other federal programs.

Individuals entering the work force should have the right to choose whether they will sign up for Social Security taxes and benefits, or instead private retirement and pension programs, either at their place of employment or independently.

We call for the removal of earning limitations on persons aged 62 and over, so that they may earn any amount of additional income they choose, without placing their Social Security benefits at risk.

We urge the repeal of those provisions of the Social Security system which penalize those born during the "notch years" between 1917 and 1926 and argue that such persons be placed on the same benefit schedules as all other beneficiaries.

TARIFFS AND TRADE

Article I, Section 8 of the Constitution says the Congress shall have power "to regulate Commerce with foreign Nations."

Congress may not abdicate or transfer to others its constitutional functions. We, therefore, oppose the unconstitutional transfer of authority over U.S. trade policy from the Congress to agencies, domestic and foreign, which improperly exercise policy setting functions with respect to U.S. trade policy.

We also favor the abolition of the Office of Special Trade Representative and insist on the withdrawal of the United States from the General Agreement on Tariffs and Trade (GATT) and all other agreements wherein bureaucracies, institutions, or individuals, other than the Congress of the United States, improperly assume responsibility for establishing policies which directly affect the economic well-being of every American citizen.

As indicated in Article I, Section 8, duties, imposts, and excises are legitimate revenue-raising measures on which the United States government may properly rely. As Abraham Lincoln pointed out, the legitimate costs of the federal government can be borne, either by taxes on American citizens and businesses, or by tariffs on foreign companies and products. The latter is preferable to the former.

Similarly, we oppose other international trade agreements which have the effect of diminishing America's economic self-sufficiency and of exporting jobs, the loss of which will impoverish American families, undermine American communities, and diminish America's capacity for economic self-reliance.

We see our country and its workers as more than bargaining chips for multi-national corporations and international banks in their ill- and evilly-conceived New World Order.

The defense of the American nation and the preservation of its economic integrity is essential to the defense of the liberty and prosperity of every American citizen.

We will recommend strict federal criminal penalties for any officer of the United States government who subsequently hires himself or herself out to represent any foreign government or other entity, public or private, with respect to influencing either public opinion or public policy on matters affecting U.S. trade with any such governments or other entities.

The indebtedness of the American government has dangerously contributed to making our economy more vulnerable to foreign takeover and manipulation. Particularly in the area of national security, foreign interests have thus been abetted in gaining access to America's high-tech secrets under the guise of commercial enterprise.

We reject the concept of Most-Favored-Nation status, especially insofar as it has been used to curry favor with regimes whose domestic and international policies are abhorrent to decent people everywhere and are in fundamental conflict with the vital interests of the United States of America.

TAXATION

The Constitution, in Article I, Section 8, gives Congress the power "to lay and collect Taxes, Duties, Imposts, and Excises, to pay the Debts and provide for the common Defence and general Welfare of the United States."

In Article I, Section 9, the original document made clear that "no Capitation, or other direct, Tax shall be laid, unless in Proportion to the Census or Enumeration herein before directed to be taken." It is moreover established that "No Tax or Duty shall be laid on Articles exported from any State."

Since 1913, our constitutional rights to life, liberty, and property have been abridged and diminished by the assumption of direct taxing authority on each of us by the federal government.

We will propose legislation to abolish the Internal Revenue Service and will veto any authorization, appropriation, or continuing resolution which contains any funding whatsoever for that illicit and unconstitutional agency.

Moreover, it is our intention to replace entirely the current tax system of the U.S. government (including income taxes, Social Security taxes, estate taxes, inheritance taxes, corporate taxes, and fuel taxes) with a new approach based on the original design of our Founding Fathers.

To the degree that tariffs on foreign products are insufficient to cover the legitimate constitutional costs of the federal government, we will offer a "state rate tax" in which the responsibility for covering the cost of unmet obligations will be divided among the several states in accordance with their proportion of the total population of the United States, excluding the District of Columbia. Thus, if a state contains 10 percent of the nation's citizens, it will be responsible for assuming payment of 10 percent of the annual deficit.

The effect of this "state rate tax" will be to encourage politicians to argue for less rather than more federal spending.

VETO AUTHORITY

Article I, Section 9 of the Constitution says: "No money shall be drawn from the Treasury, but in Consequence of Appropriations made by Law." Appropriations can be made in only two circumstances: a) either a money measure shall be passed by Congress and signed into law by the President, or b) a money measure shall be enacted over a President's veto.

A President who enjoys the support of one-third plus one of the members of either House of Congress has the constitutional authority to stop unwise and excessive federal spending.

We urge the President of the United States to use his veto power to terminate funding for all federal departments, agencies, and regulatory authorities which exist or operate beyond the bounds of the U.S. Constitution.

We specifically urge the President elected in 1992 to veto any appropriation bill which authorizes outlays in excess of $1 trillion.

WELFARE

The God Who endows us with life, liberty, property, and the right to pursue happiness also charges us to care for the needy, the sick, the homeless, the aged, and those who are otherwise unable to care for themselves.

Charity, and the provision of welfare to those in need, is not a responsibility of the federal government. It may be more efficiently and effectively provided by other entities.

Until the 1960s, it was understood and well recognized that bureaucrats in the nation's capital are unable to make proper decisions concerning welfare policy in communities far distant from them. The more remote the source of charity, the less effective and appropriate the action and the smaller the portion which reaches the needy.

More important, the effect of welfare is determined by the context in which it is delivered. The message of Christian charity is fundamentally at odds with the concept of welfare rights. In many cases, the delivery of welfare by government is not only misdirected, but morally destructive.

To a very great degree, America's welfare crisis is a government-induced crisis. Government social and cultural policies have undermined the work ethic, even as the government's economic and regulatory policies have undermined the ability of our citizens to obtain work.

We encourage individuals and families to fulfill their personal responsibility to help those in need through tithes, offerings, and other acts of charity.

The nation's churches and synagogues should manifest their faith by supporting effective programs to assist those who are in need.

Under no circumstances should the taxpayers of the United States be obliged, under penalty of law and through forced taxation, to assume the cost of providing welfare to able-bodied individuals. Nor should taxpayers be indentured to subsidize welfare for persons who enter the United States illegally.

It is the intended purpose of civil government to safeguard our lives, liberty, and property—not to redistribute our wealth. The Bible commands, "Thou shalt not steal." Theft is wrong, even when it is achieved in elegant surroundings during broad daylight and by majority vote.

Book Order Form

☐ Please send ____ additional copies of *The Next Four Years*.

☐ My check for $_____ is enclosed, payable to Policy Analysis, Inc.

☐ Please charge my Visa / MasterCard (circle one)

_____   _____

Card Number   Expiration Date

_____

Signature

_____

Name

_____

Address

_____

City, State, Zip Code

_____

Phone (optional)

Pricing

1 copy	$ 10.00
2-10 copies	$ 9.00 each
11-25 copies	$ 8.00 each
26-100 copies	$ 6.00 each
101-250 copies	$ 5.00 each
251 or more copies	$ 4.00 each

(Please add 7% of total order for postage and handling. $2.50 minimum; $15.00 maximum.)

Please send your order with payment to:

Circulation Manager
Policy Analysis, Inc.
9520 Bent Creek Lane
Vienna, Virginia 22182

Taxpayers for Phillips
9520 Bent Creek Lane
Vienna, Virginia 22182

❑ I want Howard Phillips to have the funds needed to continue his political action activities.

❑ Enclosed is my most generous possible contribution of:

❑$50 ❑$100 ❑$35 ❑$25 ❑$250 ❑$1000
❑ other $_____

❑ I have made my check payable to *Taxpayers for Phillips*.　❑ Charge the above contribution to my:

_____
Name

_____
Address

_____
City　　　State　　　Zip

_____
Phone (optional)

❑ Visa　　❑ MasterCard

Acc't #_____

Exp.date_____

_____
Signature

The Federal Election Commission
requires us to report the following:

Your occupation:_____

Name of employer:_____

Contributions are not tax deductible. Federal law prohibits corporate gifts. Each family member can contribute up to a maximum of $2,000 apiece--- $1,000 for primaries, $1,000 for the general election.

Paid for by *Taxpayers for Phillips*, Mark A. Weaver, Treasurer.
9520 Bent Creek Lane • Vienna, Virginia 22182